OECD *Economic Surveys*
Electronic Books

The OECD, recognising the strategic role of electronic publishing, will be issuing the OECD *Economic Surveys*, both for the Member countries and for countries of Central and Eastern Europe covered by the Organisation's Centre for Co-operation with Economies in Transition, as electronic books with effect from the 1994/1995 series -- incorporating the text, tables and figures of the printed version. The information will appear on screen in an identical format, including the use of colour in graphs.

The electronic book, which retains the quality and readability of the printed version throughout, will enable readers to take advantage of the new tools that the ACROBAT software (included on the diskette) provides by offering the following benefits:

❏ User-friendly and intuitive interface
❏ Comprehensive index for rapid text retrieval, including a table of contents, as well as a list of numbered tables and figures
❏ Rapid browse and search facilities
❏ Zoom facility for magnifying graphics or for increasing page size for easy readability
❏ Cut and paste capabilities
❏ Printing facility
❏ Reduced volume for easy filing/portability

Working environment: DOS, Windows or Macintosh.

Subscription: FF 1 800   US$317   £200   DM 545

Single issue: FF 130   US$24   £14   DM 40

Complete 1994/1995 series on CD-ROM:

FF 2 000   US$365   £220   DM 600

Please send your order to OECD Electronic Editions or, preferably, to the Centre or bookshop with whom you placed your initial order for this Economic Survey.

OECD
ECONOMIC
SURVEYS

1994-1995

SWITZERLAND

ORGANISATION FOR ECONOMIC CO-OPERATION AND DEVELOPMENT

ORGANISATION FOR ECONOMIC CO-OPERATION AND DEVELOPMENT

Pursuant to Article 1 of the Convention signed in Paris on 14th December 1960, and which came into force on 30th September 1961, the Organisation for Economic Co-operation and Development (OECD) shall promote policies designed:

— to achieve the highest sustainable economic growth and employment and a rising standard of living in Member countries, while maintaining financial stability, and thus to contribute to the development of the world economy;

— to contribute to sound economic expansion in Member as well as non-member countries in the process of economic development; and

— to contribute to the expansion of world trade on a multilateral, non-discriminatory basis in accordance with international obligations.

The original Member countries of the OECD are Austria, Belgium, Canada, Denmark, France, Germany, Greece, Iceland, Ireland, Italy, Luxembourg, the Netherlands, Norway, Portugal, Spain, Sweden, Switzerland, Turkey, the United Kingdom and the United States. The following countries became Members subsequently through accession at the dates indicated hereafter: Japan (28th April 1964), Finland (28th January 1969), Australia (7th June 1971), New Zealand (29th May 1973) and Mexico (18th May 1994). The Commission of the European Communities takes part in the work of the OECD (Article 13 of the OECD Convention).

Publié également en français.

3 2280 00481 3739

Table of contents

Introduction   1

I.   Recent trends and short-term prospects   3

The early phase of the current upswing   3
Further losses in employment   9
Declining unemployment   11
The size of the output gap   16
Attaining a stable price level   16
Robust exports and soaring imports   25
The outlook to 1996   32

II.   Economic policy   36

Monetary policy   36
Fiscal policy   52
Structural policies   65

III.   Public sector efficiency and management   68

Introduction   68
General government sector   69
Public enterprises   81
Assessment   104

IV.   Conclusions   107

Notes   114

References   124

Annex

Calendar of main economic events   127

Statistical annex and structural indicators   131

Boxes

1. The price effect of VAT   23
2. Overview of the 1995 revisions to monetary statistics   50
3. Outsourcing   76
4. Public enterprises of the canton of Bern   79

Tables

Text

1. Household appropriation account   7
2. Level and structure of recent unemployment   12
3. Indicators of the "natural rate" of unemployment   15
4. Price trends   20
5. Foreign trade by commodity group   27
6. Balance of payments   31
7. Short-term projections   34
8. Monetary aggregates   39
9. Nominal and real interest rates in selected OECD countries   45
10. The 1990-94 base money targeting exercise   47
11. Resetting the medium-term monetary target for the 1995-99 period   48
12. Government accounts   53
13. Central government budget   55
14. Composition and growth in the Confederation's expenditure, 1995   57
15. Composition and growth in the Confederation's receipts, 1995   58
16. The 1994 consolidation programme of the Confederation   61
17. Growth in expenditures and revenues of the Confederation to 1998   63
18. Social welfare expenditure   64
19. Share of general government in total employment   71

20.	Current outlays, 1994	72
21.	Method of service provision	78
22.	Financial accounts of the Swiss PTT, 1994	85
23.	Status of facilities competition in the OECD area, 1994	88
24.	Mainline penetration and universal service provision	89
25.	Leased line connections as a percentage of telecommunications mainlines	91
26.	Charges for telecommunications services in Switzerland	91
27.	Series index of business "telecommunications basket" total charges	92
28.	Efficiency measures of European railways, 1962-88	95
29.	Efficiency decomposition into managerial and regulatory efficiency	96

Statistical annex and structural indicators

A.	Selected background statistics	132
B.	Gross national product, current prices	133
C.	Gross national product, 1980 prices	134
D.	Producer and import prices	135
E.	Money supply	136
F.	Interest rates and capital markets	137
G.	Foreign trade by area	138
H.	Foreign trade by commodity group	139
I.	Balance of payments	140
J.	Gross value added by main area of activity	141
K.	Labour market: structural and institutional characteristics	142
L.	The structure of taxation	143
M.	Interest rate margins in banking	144

Figures

Text

1.	Output and investment: an international comparison	4
2.	Contribution to real GDP growth	8
3.	Output, labour force and employment	10

4.   Total and long-term unemployment   14

5.   The output gap   17

6.   International comparison of consumer prices   18

7.   Indicators of underlying inflation   21

8.   Labour cost and productivity   24

9.   Competitiveness and trade   26

10.   Regional disaggregation of changes in exports   29

11.   Foreign trade indicators   30

12.   Indicators of activity   33

13.   The adjusted monetary base   38

14.   Interest rates   41

15.   Exchange rates   42

16.   International comparison of long-term interest rates   43

17.   Budget balances and debt   54

18.   Trends in current outlays in Switzerland   70

19.   Ownership of industries in selected OECD countries   82

20.   Quality of service in selected Member countries   90

21.   Total telecommunications charges: competitive versus
non-competitive systems   93

22.   Electricity prices and taxes for households, 1993   98

23.   Electricity prices and taxes for industry, 1993   99

24.   Premiums relative to pay-outs for fire insurance   101

25.   Market share of the cantonal banks   103

BASIC STATISTICS OF SWITZERLAND

THE LAND

Area (1 000 sq. km)	41.3	Major cities, 1993 estimates	
Cultivated land, grassland and pastures		(1 000 inhabitants):	
(1 000 sq. km) 1979/85	15.8	Zurich	355.3
Forest (1 000 sq. km) 1979/85	12.5	Basle	180.0
		Geneva	173.5
		Bern	135.1

THE PEOPLE

Population, December 31, 1993, estimates		Number of foreign workers (1 000), end of	
(1 000)	6 969	August 1994	946.7
Number of persons per sq.km	169	Average increase in the number of foreign	
Net annual rate of population increase		workers census, end of August (1 000):	
(per 1 000 inhabitants, average 1990-93)	11	1962-72	16.8
Civilian employment, 1994 (1 000)	3 330	1973-93	2.5
Percentage distribution:			
Agriculture	5.6		
Industry and construction	33.0		
Other activities	61.4		

PRODUCTION

Gross domestic product in 1994		Value added by origin in 1990	
(billion Swiss francs)	356.2	(in per cent of GDP at factor cost):	
Growth of real GDP, 1990-94 average		Agriculture	3.1
(annual rate, per cent)	0.2	Industry	26.3
Real gross fixed investment in 1994		Construction	8.4
(in per cent of GDP)	28.2	Services	62.2
Growth of real investment, 1990-94 average			
(annual rate, per cent)	−1.1		

THE GOVERNMENT [1]

Public consumption in 1994 (in per cent		Composition of Parliament (in per cent):	
of GDP)	14.3		National Council	State Council
Revenue of the Confederation in 1994			
(in per cent of GDP)	10.2	Radical Democrats	22.0	39.1
Total debt in 1994 (in per cent of GDP)	46.7	Christian Democrats	18.5	34.8
		Socialists	21.5	6.5
		Central Democratic Union	12.5	8.7
		Other	25.5	10.9
		Last elections: 1991		
		Next elections: 1995		

FOREIGN TRADE

Exports of goods and services as a percentage		Imports of goods and services as a percentage	
of GDP (average 1990-94)	36.1	of GDP (average 1990-94)	33.0
Commodity exports (fob, million Swiss francs,		Commodity imports (cif, million Swiss francs,	
1994)	90 213	1994)	87 279
Percentage distribution:		Percentage distribution:	
By area in 1994		By area in 1994	
To OECD countries	78.7	From OECD countries	90.9
To EEC countries	62.7	From EEC countries	80.3
To OPEC countries	3.2	From OPEC countries	1.3
By categories in 1994		By categories in 1994	
Raw materials and semi-finished goods	29.4	Raw materials and semi-finished goods	31.4
Capital goods	34.8	Energy	3.5
Consumer goods	35.8	Capital goods	25.6
		Consumer goods	39.5

THE CURRENCY

Monetary unit: Swiss franc		Currency unit per US$, average of daily	
		figures:	
		Year 1994	1.3671
		June 1995	1.1561

1. Confederation, cantons and communes.

Note: An international comparison of certain statistics is given in an annex table.

This Survey is based on the Secretariat's study prepared for the annual review of Switzerland by the Economic and Development Review Committee on 26th June 1995.

•

After revisions in the light of discussions during the review, final approval of the Survey for publication was given by the Committee on 10th July 1995.

•

The previous Survey of Switzerland was issued in August 1994.

Introduction

Switzerland's economy bottomed out during the summer of 1993, ending the longest recession in the post-war period. Tight monetary policy, slack in economic activity and an appreciating Swiss franc brought inflation down from a peak of 6½ per cent in the summer of 1991 to around ½ per cent during most of 1994. As a consequence of the economic slump, employment declined substantially from 1991 to 1994 and unemployment rose until the end of 1993, to levels never seen before in Switzerland. The expansion since the second half of 1993 has been led by a turnaround in fixed investment, strong inventory accumulation and accelerating exports, with real GDP growing by just over 2 per cent in 1994. However, the fall in employment came to a halt only in the second half of 1994. Recent macroeconomic trends are discussed in Chapter I of this Survey, together with economic projections to 1996.

The challenge to economic policy now is to promote high and sustained growth in order to create jobs, while locking in the achieved price stability. This requires prudent macroeconomic policies. Despite the recent decline in short-term interest rates, monetary policy appears to be cautious. Thus, the Survey argues that, if the strength of the Swiss franc and the slow growth of monetary aggregates persist, there would be a case for further monetary relaxation. The contribution of fiscal policy to macroeconomic stabilisation is to curtail the sizeable non-cyclical part of the general government deficit in order to make room for more private investment. By keeping the stock of government debt small, this would help maintain the flexibility of fiscal policies needed in future cyclical downturns. Macroeconomic policies should be complemented by microeconomic reform measures aimed at intensifying competition in the domestic economy, which should also make prices in the sheltered sector more responsive to monetary policy. Chapter II provides an assessment of recent developments in monetary and fiscal policy and briefly takes stock of latest initiatives in the field of microeconomic reform.

Chapter III takes a close look at the efficiency of the Swiss public sector and its management. The provision of the goods and services by the public sector is not subject to competition and therefore risks being inefficient and inattentive to clients' needs. These concerns have been sharpened by budgetary pressures on all levels of government in recent years. Finally, policy conclusions are presented in Chapter IV.

I. Recent trends and short-term prospects

The early phase of the current upswing

After three years of recession, the Swiss economy grew at an estimated rate of 2.1 per cent[1] in 1994, in line with the average of the smaller European OECD countries. Growth of real GDP slowed down, however, in the first quarter of 1995, to a seasonally-adjusted annual rate (s.a.a.r. hereafter) of about 1 per cent. Activity had already turned around in the middle of 1993, led by buoyant exports and fixed investment. Due to double-digit growth of machinery and equipment investment, fixed investment rebounded strongly in the second half of 1993, after a cumulative decline of 14½ per cent (s.a.) since the beginning of 1990. With a temporary surge in residential construction, fixed investment growth gathered strength in the first half of 1994 but decelerated markedly in the second half; a vigorous recovery of fixed investment, however, was recorded in the first quarter of 1995.

Machinery and equipment investment is estimated to have grown by 10 per cent in volume terms in 1994, raising its share in GDP to 10½ per cent, not far from the pre-recession level of 11¼ per cent; it remained extraordinarily buoyant in the first quarter of 1995. Its recent recovery compares quite favourably with developments in other OECD countries (Figure 1). As in the post-1982-recession period,[2] the current recovery of machinery and equipment investment began at a time when economic prospects were still clouded by uncertainty. Various indicators were generally pointing to still fragile economic conditions. Merchandise export volumes had been on an upward trend since the beginning of 1993 but from a depressed level and with feeble growth – an average annual rate of 0.6 per cent. The indicators for "trend of orders" and "production prospects" had recovered from their troughs in late 1992, but remained at unsatisfactory levels throughout 1993. The KOF business climate indicator eventually picked up by

Figure 1. **OUTPUT AND INVESTMENT: AN INTERNATIONAL COMPARISON**

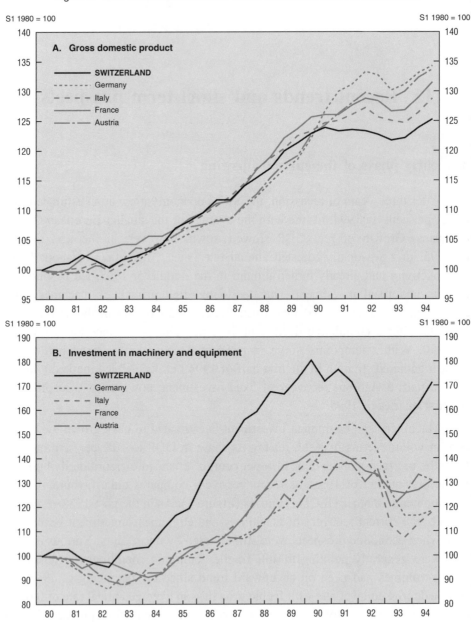

S1 1980 = 100

A. Gross domestic product

SWITZERLAND
Germany
Italy
France
Austria

S1 1980 = 100

B. Investment in machinery and equipment

SWITZERLAND
Germany
Italy
France
Austria

Source: OECD.

4

mid-1993, but entered the "normal" range only at the end of 1993. Industrial capacity utilisation started to improve in the spring of 1993 from a low of 79 per cent and attained its long-term average of 84½ per cent only by the end of 1994. And real long-term interest rates had come down in 1993, but rose in 1994 to high levels compared with earlier periods of recovery (see Chapter II below).

The strength of machinery and equipment investment in this environment largely reflected the underlying need to modernise the business capital stock. Very moderate wage increases and substantial productivity gains gave a boost to company profitability. Damped prices of imported investment goods ensuing from the appreciating Swiss franc are also likely to have contributed to demand: these prices fell by 7 per cent in 1994, after a decline of 1½ per cent in 1993. The decline in the prices of imported investment goods became even more pronounced during the first four months of 1995. Import volumes of investment goods indeed rose by 13.4 per cent in 1994 and so did their share in total machinery and equipment investment volumes – to 88 per cent in 1994 compared with 74 per cent in 1989. Purchases of office machinery, especially computers, were particularly buoyant. Demand for domestically-produced investment goods strengthened in the second half of 1994, largely as a result of purchases by the State Railway system (CFF) and the PTT. Altogether, fears voiced earlier that business capital spending could be deferred on a large scale until 1995 when the replacement of the old turnover-tax on goods by a general value-added tax (VAT) was scheduled to eliminate the tax on investment ("taxe occulte") proved to be exaggerated.

A surge in residential investment by around 10 per cent, in spite of subdued growth of household incomes, accounts for the rather unexpected increase in construction activity in 1994. It appears that residential investment has been stimulated by a combination of lower mortgage interest rates, subsidised federal housing loans, softer real-estate prices and construction costs,[3] and a back-log of housing demand built up during the recession. Excess capacity in the construction sector is also likely to have contributed. In contrast, KOF estimates[4] are for another contraction of business construction volumes by 4-5 per cent in 1994, which implies a cumulative decline of some 30 per cent over the past three years. It appears that business construction is still suffering from the large stock of unused structures accumulated in the pre-1990 real-estate boom, an interpretation which is supported by reports of sharply falling prices for commercial buildings.

5

In spite of fiscal restraint on all levels of government, public construction appears to have increased somewhat, after its decline in 1993. The modest real growth of just over 1 per cent in 1994 (KOF estimate) is largely attributable to the federal government's "investment bonus programme" which was introduced in the Spring of 1993; it makes additional construction investment or the significant advancement of already planned projects of cantons, communes and state companies eligible for a federal subsidy of 15 per cent of the construction cost, provided that the project will be finished before the middle of 1995. The volume of the "investment bonus programme" amounted to SF 200 million and has been fully allocated to around 1 000 projects which were all in progress in 1994.[5] Assessment of the impact of the investment bonus programme is, however, complicated by the uncertainty about the volume of additional projects it has induced. Especially in the case of cantons or communes which do not establish medium-term investment programmes, the distinction between additional projects and those intended anyway is difficult to make. Official estimates suggest that, after contracting by 1.7 per cent in 1993, public consumption also posted positive real growth in 1994, notwithstanding government efforts to curb budget deficits. Major sources of the volume increase of some 1½ per cent in 1994 are higher military expenditures – after substantial cuts in preceding years – and a rebound in government employment.

Private consumption also recovered in 1994, after the declines in 1992 and 1993. It recovered in spite of further falls in employment and fairly modest wage increases, which allowed total compensation of employees to grow by only 1¼ per cent in 1994, about the same rate as in 1993. Incomes from property and entrepreneurship turned around and increased by a healthy 5 per cent. But with strong growth in direct taxes,[6] disposable incomes are estimated to have grown by some 1 per cent in 1994 and to have broadly stagnated in real terms. This implies another fall in the household saving ratio, for the third year in a row, by nearly 1 percentage point to about 11 per cent in 1994 (Table 1). Hence, during the recent recession and the first year of the current upswing, the falling savings ratio was a more important stabilising factor of activity than in earlier comparable episodes.

The turnaround in real consumer expenditures was mainly due to purchases of durables, in particular automobiles and household appliances, for which there may have been pent-up demand for replacement after two years of decreasing

6

Table 1. **Household appropriation account**

	1989 at current prices	Percentage change from previous period				
		1990	1991	1992	1993	1994[1]
Compensation of employees	174 295	8.9	7.3	3.4	1.0	1.2
Entrepreneurial income	27 165	2.2	1.5	-3.7	-1.2	5.0
Interest and dividend income	20 700	14.9	5.4	2.6	-3.4	5.0
Rent income	1 235	-1.2	4.1	4.7	10.9	0.0
Primary income	223 395	8.6	6.5	2.5	0.4	1.9
Current transfers received	47 305	9.5	12.3	12.0	10.9	3.3
Total income	270 700	8.7	7.5	4.3	2.5	2.2
less: Current transfers paid (including direct taxes)	83 960	9.6	5.9	5.8	5.1	4.5
Disposable income	186 740	8.3	8.2	3.6	1.3	1.1
Household consumption	166 150	6.9	7.2	4.0	2.1	2.1
Savings	20 590					
Household savings ratio in per cent of disposable income	11.0	12.2	13.0	12.7	12.0	11.1
Real disposable income		2.9	2.4	-0.5	-1.6	0.2

1. OECD estimates.
Source: Office fédéral de la statistique, *Comptes nationaux de la Suisse 1993;* OECD.

real household expenditures. Tourism spending abroad was also very buoyant, while residents' tourism activity inside Switzerland remained sluggish, reflecting a relative price effect induced by the appreciation of the Swiss franc. The growth in household consumption (s.a.) was particularly pronounced in the first half of 1994, while later on it weakened and seems to have fallen in the fourth quarter of the year; it seems to have recovered again in the first quarter of 1995. This is in some contrast to the development of the consumer confidence indicator which had bottomed out in late 1992 and has since kept rising until the end of 1994. However, a deterioration of consumer confidence has been registered in the first quarter of 1995, probably due to a fall in real disposable incomes ensuing from the introduction of VAT and increased social security contributions.

Exports of goods and services, which had initially helped to pull the economy out of recession, stagnated in the first half of 1994, before regaining their dynamism in the second half-year. The recovery of exports and domestic demand, combined with steeply falling import prices induced by exchange rate

7

Figure 2. **CONTRIBUTION TO REAL GDP GROWTH**

As a percentage of GDP in the previous year

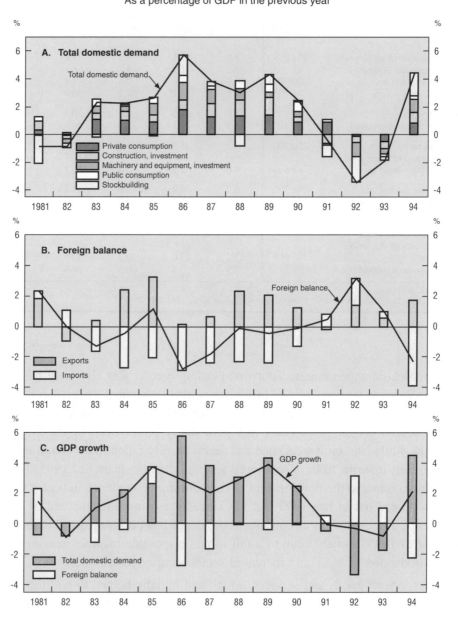

Source: OECD, *National Accounts.*

appreciation, caused import volumes to surge, so that the contribution of the real foreign balance to GDP growth turned negative in 1994 (Figure 2). Seasonally-adjusted exports of goods and services decreased in the first quarter of 1995 of an annual rate of about –7 per cent, while the strong growth of total imports even accelerated, making for a strong negative contribution of the real foreign balance to GDP growth.

Thanks to the marked turnaround of domestic demand and strengthening exports, value added[7] of all major sectors of the economy picked up in 1994, for the first time since 1990. Industrial value added expanded by 2.5 per cent, which was even surpassed by the 3³/₄ per cent gain in value added in the construction sector. In contrast, value added of the services sector advanced by only about 1 per cent in 1994, depressed by a decline in tourism. The performance of the banking sector also seems to have weakened, following a very successful 1993.

Further losses in employment[8]

Employment, responding to the current recovery of output with a longer lag than experienced in previous upswings,[9] continued to fall – on a seasonally adjusted basis – until mid-1994 (Figure 3). The improvement in the second half of 1994 was too feeble to prevent a further decrease of 1.8 per cent (some 60 000 persons) in average annual employment for 1994.[10] A further fall in employment, by 1.4 per cent (s.a.a.r.), was recorded in the first quarter of 1995. The loss of jobs was most pronounced in industry (–4.2 per cent),[11] which is in stark contrast to the KOF-estimate of a 2¹/₂ per cent increase in industrial value added[12] and implies a productivity gain of nearly 7 per cent. This is also consistent with the stagnation in industrial employment during the second half of 1994 and the further fall by 2 per cent (s.a.a.r.) in the first quarter of 1995.

The improvement in employment in the second half of 1994 was largely due to the increase in newly created jobs in the construction sector, where employment expanded at a brisk 4³/₄ per cent pace (s.a.a.r.); however, it decreased steeply in the first quarter of 1995, by 12¹/₂ per cent (s.a.a.r.). Some branches of the services sector also recorded employment gains, such as social services, health and insurance – activities which tend to be sheltered from foreign competition. The major part of the services sector as well as the manufacturing sector reported no or only small employment gains in the second half of 1994.

Figure 3. **OUTPUT, LABOUR FORCE AND EMPLOYMENT**

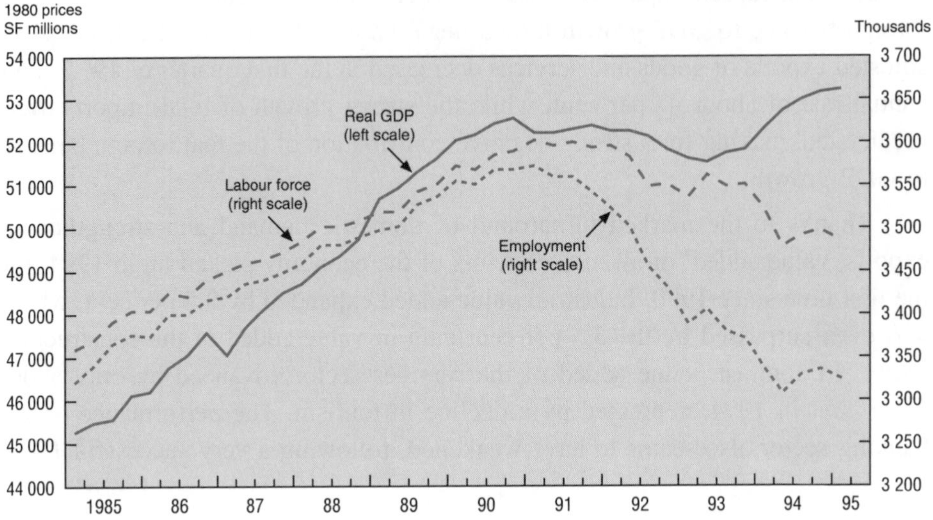

1980 prices
SF millions

Thousands

Source: KOF/ETH, *Konjunktur.*

The cumulative decline of 1.2 per cent in aggregate output during the recession was accompanied by a fall in total employment of 6.5 per cent below its peak reached in 1990, equivalent to the loss of some 233 000 jobs.[13] Although industrial value-added contracted by less than 3 per cent during the recession, about 12 per cent of the pre-recession employment in industry – or some 106 thousand jobs – has been cut over the 1990-94 period;[14] this nearly accounts for half of the total fall in employment. The decline in employment in construction over the same period was equally steep in relative terms. On the other hand and similar to other OECD economies, the services sector fared relatively better during the recession, with a cumulative decrease in employment of 3.6 per cent (–77 000 jobs).[15] In relative terms, women and men were about equally hit by the fall in employment during the cyclical downturn,[16] but this time foreigners were much less affected by job losses than Swiss nationals.[17] Of the foreign labour force, seasonal workers bore the brunt of the recession, their number halving from 120 thousand to 60 thousand between 1990 and 1994. Employment of frontier workers still increased in 1991, but fell thereafter by some 15 per cent to 153 thousand in 1994.

Declining unemployment

Notwithstanding the continuing decline in employment until the middle of 1994, the seasonally adjusted rate of registered unemployment peaked at 5 per cent of the total labour force in December 1993 and January 1994 and from then on fell very gradually to 4.2 per cent in May 1995. Due to a carry-over effect, the average annual rate of 4.7 per cent in 1994 was slightly above that in 1993. The fall in unemployment in the first half of 1994 was due to a contraction of the labour force in excess of employment losses. The labour participation rate fell by about 3/4 percentage point in 1994 to 67.1 per cent. One cause of this is a growing participation in education and training, partly because employment prospects are bleak. Another factor is that people who have reached unemployment benefit termination – currently after 400 days – might have chosen not to register any longer with the labour office, thereby dropping out of the labour force statistics.[18]

With the indigenous labour force falling faster than the foreign workforce in 1994, the unemployment rate of foreigners (8.4 per cent) remained much higher than that of Swiss nationals (3.7 per cent), in spite of employment losses for foreigners being substantially smaller than those for Swiss citizens[19] (Table 2). The continued growth of the foreign workforce during the recession and its near-stabilisation in 1994 contrasts with the shrinking Swiss labour force. In part, this is due to the ongoing practice of converting seasonal work permits into annual ones, which then also gives the foreign worker's family the right to move to Switzerland. The much higher unemployment rate of foreigners appears to be correlated with a generally lower level of qualification than that of Swiss workers.

The unemployment rate of the very young (15 to 19 years) remained below 2 per cent, while the high rate of the group of 20 to 24 years only declined by 0.2 percentage point to 6.1 per cent in 1994. However, a substantial decrease in unemployment of the latter age group was recorded in the course of 1994 and in the first quarter of 1995, to a rate of 4.8 per cent in May. On the other hand, the rate of unemployment of those aged 50 and more rose by 3/4 percentage point to an average of 4.2 per cent in 1994; only a small improvement was visible in the Spring of 1995.

A salient feature of the Swiss labour market is the sharp increase in long-term (defined as more than one year) unemployment since 1990, the first year it

Table 2. Level and structure of recent unemployment

	1991 Number	1991 Rate[1]	1992 Number	1992 Rate[1]	1993 Number	1993 Rate[1]	1994 Number	1994 Rate[1]	1995 Q1 Number	1995 Q1 Rate[1]	1995 April/May Number	1995 April/May Rate[1]
Total	39 222	1.1	92 308	2.5	163 135	4.5	171 038	4.7	160 774	4.4	154 321	4.2
According to region												
German speaking	18 889	0.7	51 565	2.0	96 959	3.7	99 463	3.8	89 470	3.4	85 990	3.2
French and Italian speaking	20 333	2.0	40 743	4.0	66 176	6.5	71 574	7.1	71 304	7.1	68 331	6.7
According to gender												
Women	16 507	1.2	37 591	2.7	66 571	4.7	73 072	5.2	69 733	4.9	67 702	4.8
Men	22 715	1.0	54 717	2.5	96 564	4.4	97 966	4.4	91 041	4.1	86 619	3.9
According to citizenship												
Swiss	22 370	0.8	55 636	2.0	99 631	3.5	102 757	3.7	93 149	3.3	89 333	3.1
Foreign	16 852	2.1	36 672	4.5	63 504	7.8	68 281	8.4	67 625	8.3	64 988	8.0
According to age												
15-24 years	7 377	1.1	19 883	3.0	32 098	4.9	30 831	4.7	25 334	3.8	23 975	3.6
25-49 years	25 613	1.2	58 480	2.7	103 459	4.8	107 410	4.9	102 334	4.7	98 328	4.5
50 years and more	6 232	0.8	13 945	1.8	27 578	3.5	32 797	4.2	33 106	4.2	32 018	4.5
According to sectors *(Share in %)*												
Agriculture	317	0.2	827	0.4	1 522	0.8	1 590	0.8	1 704	1.2	1 673	0.7
Energy, mining	83	0.3	234	0.9	448	1.8	523	2.1	522	2.1	512	2.1
Arts and crafts, industry	10 408	1.2	24 623	3.0	40 916	5.1	40 146	4.6	33 355	3.8	31 876	3.6
Construction	3 510	1.1	9 504	3.0	17 441	5.1	16 455	4.8	15 709	5.0	16 365	4.2
Distributive trade, catering, repairs	10 604	1.3	24 154	3.0	42 437	5.5	46 889	5.7	45 981	5.6	44 739	5.5
Transport and communication	1 288	0.6	3 089	1.4	5 183	2.4	5 363	2.5	4 766	2.2	4 591	2.1
Banking, insurance, consultancy	6 068	1.4	13 370	3.1	20 970	4.9	20 395	4.6	18 945	4.3	18 180	4.1
Other services	4 986	0.9	11 624	2.2	18 827	3.6	21 650	4.2	21 522	4.2	21 079	4.1
Government	918	0.7	2 321	1.7	3 784	2.8	4 362	3.4	5 595	3.6	6 015	4.0
Not specified[2]	1 042	–	2 562	–	11 607	–	13 665	–	12 675	–	11 493	–
According to duration *(Share in %)*												
0-6 months	30 245	77.1	60 633	65.7	85 667	52.3	73 651	43.0	75 187	46.8	68 770	44.5

Specialists	17 147	43.7	43 764	47.4	80 152	49.1	85 240	48.7	77 258	48.0	74 185	46.1
Auxiliaries	18 761	47.8	39 170	42.4	64 327	39.4	65 981	38.6	63 883	39.7	61 598	39.9
Apprentices/students	1 173	3.0	4 449	4.8	9 936	6.1	11 995	7.0	10 237	6.4	9 259	6.0
Other	2 141	5.5	4 925	5.4	8 740	5.4	9 816	5.7	9 416	5.9	9 279	6.0

1. Official unemployment statistics include those who are partially unemployed. With the exception of sectoral unemployment rates, official unemployment rates are expressed as a percentage of the work-force in the 1990 population census; sectoral unemployment rates are expressed as a percentage of the work-force in the corresponding period.
2. Persons seeking employment for the first time or re-entering the work-force.

Source: Office fédéral de l'industrie, des arts et métiers et du travail (unemployment), Office fédéral de la statistique (employment).

was recorded. In that year, the number of long-term unemployed was only around 1 000, but this number rose to an average of close to 50 thousand in 1994, nearly 30 per cent of total unemployment (Figure 4). Thirty per cent of the long-term unemployed are aged 50 or more; only 8 per cent of them are younger than 25 years, while these age groups' shares in total unemployment are about 20 and 16 per cent, respectively. This confirms observations that unemployment among younger age groups is primarily of a frictional and cyclical nature.

The recent sharp increase in long-term unemployment has been accompanied by a rise in estimates of the structural ("natural") rate of unemployment, which has a bearing on government finances and on the design of policies to cope with unemployment. National estimates of the structural unemployment rate ("taux de chômage incompressible") range from 1 to some 3 per cent while the Secretariat's recent estimates fall within an interval from 2 to 3½ per cent (Table 3). However, all available estimates suggest a sizeable degree of cyclical labour market slack at the present juncture, which is consistent with the notion of a substantial output gap.

Figure 4. **TOTAL AND LONG-TERM UNEMPLOYMENT**

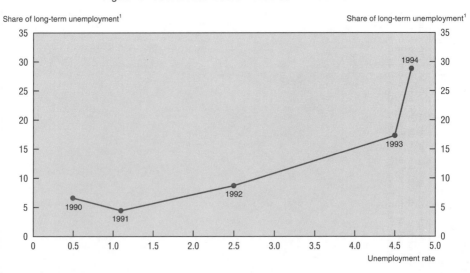

1. Unemployment for more than one year.
Source: Office fédéral de l'industrie, des arts et métiers et du travail.

Table 3. **Indicators of the "natural rate" of unemployment**

Per cent of total labour force

	1960-90	1960-69	1970-79	1980-85	1987	1988	1989	1990[1]	1991	1992	1993	1994
NAWRU[2]	–	–	0.2	0.5	0.7	0.8	1.0	1.2	1.7	2.2	2.8	3.4
Hodrick-Prescott filter[3]	0.4	0.0	0.2	0.5	0.9	1.1	1.4	1.7	2.1	2.6	3.1	3.6
Beveridge curve shift[4]	0.1	0.0	0.0	0.4	1.0	0.9	0.9	0.8	1.0	1.8	2.2	2.1
Actual unemployment rate	0.3	0.0	0.2	0.6	0.8	0.7	0.6	0.5	1.1	2.5	4.5	4.7

1. Break in series due to change in definition of unemployment rate and vacancy rate.
2. For the methodology of the non-accelerating wage rate of unemployment (NAWRU), see Elmeskov (1993).
3. The Hodrick-Prescott filter decomposes the actual unemployment rate into a smooth non-stationary component – used as approximation of the natural rate – and a stationary cyclical component. See King and Rebello (1989).
4. Calculated as exp (ln UNR + ln VAC), where UNR is the actual unemployment rate and VAC is the ratio of vacancies to the total labour force. VAC has been normalised (divided by its average value) so that ln VAC is equal to zero on average over the same period. It is assumed that the unemployment rate varies negatively with the job vacancy rate around the natural rate (UNR*) according to the following model: ln UNR = ln UNR* – ln VAC. Hence, the exponential of the sum of ln UNR and ln VAC provides an estimate of the natural rate. This estimate is also equal to the exponential of the sum of the constant term (a) and the residuals (ε) from a Beveridge curve equation as follows: ln UNR = a + b ln VAC + ε.

Source: OECD estimates.

15

The size of the output gap

With the economy now recovering from the recession and a continuation of the upswing in prospect, the question arises as to the size of the existing slack in aggregate capacity, as this has a bearing on future inflation and the setting of economic policies. A simple statistical approach[20] suggests that actual output was still some 3 per cent below potential at the end of 1994 (Figure 5). On the basis of the projections laid out below, the gap between the levels of actual and potential output (output gap) would still amount to 2³/₄ per cent by the end of 1996. A more sophisticated trending technique[21] yields a markedly smaller output gap in 1994, some 1¹/₂ per cent only; it suggests that the gap could close in the second half of 1996.

However, such simple approaches ignore the movements in factors of production. Potential output growth is likely to have slowed during the recession, given that the steep fall in both machinery and equipment and business construction investment induced a slowdown of the growth of the business capital stock from an estimated 4¹/₂ per cent in 1990 – just before the recession – to 2³/₄ per cent in 1993; it accelerated to around 3 per cent in 1994. Together with the recorded growth in the Swiss population and estimates of the trend labour participation rate, an aggregate production function estimated by the Secretariat suggests that potential output growth may have slowed in recent years, to below 1¹/₂ per cent in 1993, before improving to 1³/₄ per cent in 1994. This would imply a gap of about 2¹/₂ per cent of potential in 1993, narrowing to 2 per cent in 1994 and staying at 1³/₄ per cent of potential output in 1996.

Attaining a stable price level

The recent process of disinflation was long and painful. Although the twelve-monthly rate of consumer price inflation declined quite rapidly from its peak of 6.6 per cent reached in the summer of 1992, it hovered stubbornly around a rate of 3¹/₂ per cent during the 16 consecutive months ending in October 1993. Major causes of stalling disinflation during this period were sticky service prices – in particular rents and administered prices – and an increase in the customs duty on gasoline in March 1993. But from late 1993 onward, inflation fell rapidly to about ¹/₂ per cent in May 1994, where it stayed for the remainder of the year.

Figure 5. **THE OUTPUT GAP**

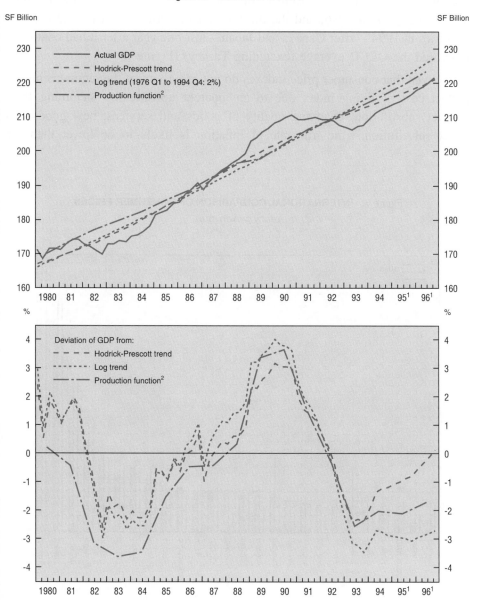

1. 1995 and 1996 are projections.
2. Yearly series.
Source: OECD.

For 1994 on average, the consumer price index (CPI) rose by 0.9 per cent, about the same rate as in 1986, and the third-lowest increase among OECD member countries in 1994 – after Canada and Japan – just one year after it had continued to exceed the OECD average (excluding Turkey) (Figure 6).

Given that consumer price indexes do not exactly meet the requirement of a perfect cost of living index due to an inherent upward bias stemming from product substitution, changing quality of goods and services, new goods and outlet substitution,[22] the true rate of inflation is likely to be lower than the

Figure 6. **INTERNATIONAL COMPARISON OF CONSUMER PRICES**
Yearly growth rates

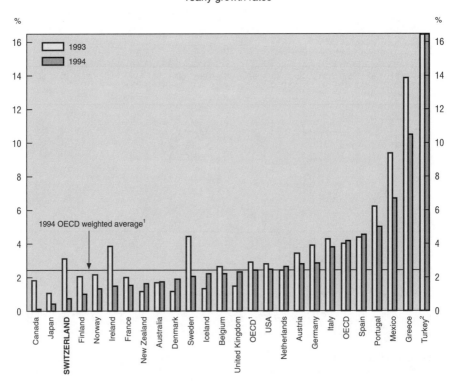

1.   OECD less Turkey.
2.   66.1 for 1993 and 106.3 for 1994.
Source: OECD, *Main Economic Indicators.*

measured change in the CPI. Although there are no empirical studies which seek to quantify this bias in Switzerland, it seems plausible to assume that it is of a magnitude similar to those found for different CPI components in other countries. Fischer and Zurlinden (1994) report on an approach which attaches the weights of the Swiss CPI to estimates of measurement biases from abroad. The resulting estimate of a total upward bias of 0.9 per cent suggests that Switzerland may have achieved a broadly stable price level in 1994.

Owing to the appreciating Swiss franc, prices of imported consumer goods and services even fell by ½ per cent in 1994 (Table 4). But at 1.3 per cent, inflation of home-produced goods and services also came rather close to the National Bank's overall inflation objective of roughly 1 per cent. A particularly gratifying feature of last year's inflation picture was the slowing of average service price increases (accounting for about 56 per cent of the CPI) to 1.4 per cent. The marked divergence of inflation rates across major CPI categories seen earlier accordingly largely levelled off in 1994. A major contribution to this came from the deceleration of rent increases, from 5.1 per cent in 1993 to only 0.6 per cent in 1994, due to stable mortgage rates[23] throughout 1994; rents even fell during the second half of 1994 and in the first four months of 1995 (Figure 7). Public service prices also decelerated, but the average increase of 2.3 per cent in 1994 is in line with earlier observations that administered prices tend to lag behind general price movements and to delay the process of disinflation.[24]

Price developments at the producer and wholesale level confirm the favourable inflation climate: in 1994, the *level* of the total supply price index as well as its two major components, the producer price index and the import price index, remained stable for the fourth successive year. Since this index includes only goods, it confirms that service prices were at the heart of the recent inflation problem. Producer prices[25] remained broadly stable during the first five months of 1995, while import prices edged up to a twelve-monthly rate of about 2 per cent, which largely reflects the strong increase of raw material prices (by 16 per cent over the 12 months to March 1995). But import price inflation decelerated to a twelve-monthly rate of 1.2 per cent in May 1995, thanks to the appreciation of the Swiss franc.

At the beginning of 1995, the old turnover tax on goods, which had left services and energy untaxed, was replaced by a general VAT on goods and services. The standard VAT rate has been set at 6.5 per cent, 0.3 percentage point

Table 4. **Price trends**

Percentage changes from previous year

	May 1993[1] Weight in %	1989	1990	1991	1992	1993	1994	1994		1995	1995
								Q3	Q4	Q1	April/May
Total supply index[2]	100.0	4.3	1.5	0.4	0.1	0.2	-0.3	-0.2	0.3	0.7	0.7
Producer price index				1.3	0.7	0.4	-0.5	-0.5	0.1	0.3	0.3
Import price index				-2.1	-1.7	-0.3	-0.1	0.6	0.7	2.0	1.2
Consumer price index	100.0	3.2	5.4	5.9	4.0	3.3	0.9	0.7	0.5	1.4	1.8
Goods	44.2	2.5	4.5	3.5	1.1	1.7	0.2	0.3	-0.1	0.5	0.5
Non-durables	25.6	2.7	4.9	3.8	0.0	1.4	0.3	0.7	0.2	1.2	1.1
of which:											
Food, beverages, tobacco	16.3	1.7	5.4	4.3	0.1	-0.1	0.5	1.3	0.6	1.3	1.3
Energy[3]	3.2	10.7	7.5	3.1	-2.6	1.2	-3.2	-2.0	-3.5	5.1	5.1
Services	55.8	3.7	6.2	8.0	6.5	4.6	1.4	0.7	0.9	2.0	2.9
of which: Rents	22.1	3.7	8.6	9.9	6.9	5.1	0.6	-0.8	-0.2	-0.4	0.5
Home produced goods and services	74.6	3.0	5.8	6.8	5.0	3.6	1.3	1.0	0.9	1.9	2.6
Imported goods and services	25.4	3.7	4.4	3.2	1.1	2.2	-0.5	-0.5	-1.0	-0.9	-0.3
Export prices[4]		7.4	1.1	2.2	1.3	1.0	-1.6	-1.0	-2.1	-4.2	..
Import prices[4]		9.0	-0.8	0.6	2.1	-1.1	-5.7	-5.1	-4.4	-5.1	..

1. Series have been rebased in May 1993.
2. The total supply price index is the total of producer and import price indices.
3. Before the first quarter of 1993: "heating and lighting".
4. Change in the price deflator of goods and services, national accounts basis.

Source: Département fédéral de l'économie publique, *La vie économique*; Banque nationale suisse, *Bulletin mensuel.*

Figure 7. **INDICATORS OF UNDERLYING INFLATION**[1]

Year-on-year change

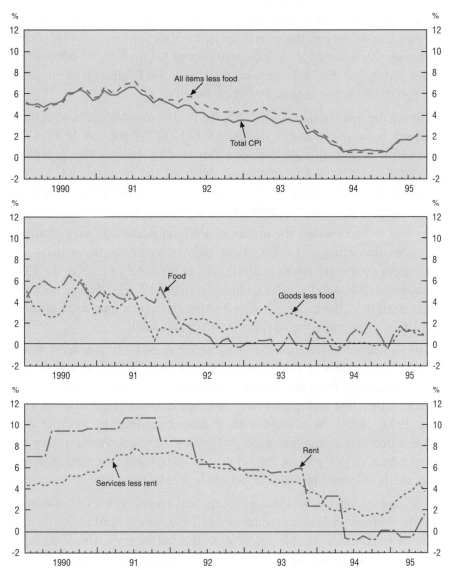

1. Weights in CPI as from May 1993 are: 0.35 for goods less food, 0.14 for food, 0.29 for services less rent and 0.22 for rent.
Source: OECD, *Main Economic Indicators.*

21

above the old standard turnover tax rate.[26] Given the preparedness of the National Bank to accommodate the VAT-induced increase in demand for money in order to avoid real output losses (see Chapter II below), this should result in a once-and-for-all rise in the consumer price level, the exact amount of which depends *inter alia* on the economy's cyclical position and the intensity of competition in different industries. Swiss estimates arrive at a VAT-induced additional CPI increase of 1 to $1\frac{1}{4}$ per cent in 1995 (see Box 1).

During the first six months of 1995, the twelve-monthly increase in the CPI accelerated, from $\frac{1}{2}$ per cent at the end of 1994 to 2.1 per cent in June.[27] The *Office fédéral de la statistique* estimates that roughly 1 percentage point of this rise is attributable to VAT, about two thirds of the mechanically calculated cumulative *direct* VAT-effect of 1.7 percentage points. This also suggests that the underlying rate of inflation remained at a low 1 per cent.

As was to be expected, the impact of VAT on prices was most pronounced for services and energy. To the extent that entrepreneurs have delayed the adjustment of their sales prices to VAT, further tax-induced rises in the CPI are to be expected. But with the price dampening indirect VAT effects – such as the elimination of the "hidden tax" – now coming through, a final extra increase in CPI-inflation of no more than $1\frac{1}{4}$ per cent appears likely.

The slowdown of price inflation was underpinned by further deceleration in nominal wage increases in 1994. This reflects the high and still rising unemployment and depressed company profits in the autumn of 1993, when most wage negotiations for 1994 had taken place. Average nominal wages rose by 1.5 per cent in 1994, below the marked gain in labour productivity (+4 per cent),[28] implying a decrease in unit labour costs (Figure 8). The concomitant steep fall in *real* unit labour costs by about $2\frac{1}{2}$ per cent is tantamount to a marked improvement in the profit share in national income in 1994.

The preparedness of workers to accept real wages which fell substantially behind the increase in labour productivity in 1994 for the third consecutive year indicates a remarkably flexible response to the fall in employment during this period. But thanks to the rapid slowdown of consumer price inflation, the real "consumption wage" still rose by an average of $\frac{1}{2}$ per cent in 1994, after the real wage loss of $\frac{3}{4}$ cent per cent in 1993. Preliminary data concerning the latest wage settlements suggest that average nominal wage increases are likely to amount to some $1\frac{1}{2}$ per cent in 1995, the same rate as in 1994. This shows that the

Box 1.   The price effect of VAT

The introduction of a general value-added tax in Switzerland has led to a rise in the consumer price level through different channels of which the most important are briefly sketched out below.

Direct effects

The tax rate on those *goods* which were taxed under the old statutory turnover tax has increased from 6.2 to 6.5 per cent.

Several formerly tax-exempt *goods* categories are now taxed at a reduced VAT-rate of 2 per cent (primarily food, non-alcoholic beverages, medication).

Previously tax-exempt *energy* and *services* are now taxed at the full rate of 6.5 per cent (housing rents, and services in the field of health, education, post, insurance and – in part – banking remain exempt).

To quantify this first-round effect, it has been assumed that the difference between the VAT rate and the previous turnover tax rate will be fully passed on to prices. Alternative estimates of the KOF (*cf.* Schnewlin and Weber, 1994) and of Zumstein (1994) arrive at a direct effect on the CPI of 1.7 percentage points, an assessment which is shared by the *Office fédéral de la statistique.*

Indirect effects

The sum of the direct effects is likely to be an upper limit of the total short-run effect because the abolition of the taxation of investment and intermediate inputs (the "taxe occulte") through VAT reduces production cost, which should at least partially be passed on to the consumer. In particular the cost reduction of intermediate inputs should quickly lower production costs whereas the "hidden tax" on investment will affect the cost of output only gradually, in line with the renewal of the capital stock. However, enterprises which are exempt from VAT will not be refunded for the VAT they paid on their inputs and are likely to try to incorporate these cost in their sales prices. Under the assumption that the abolition of the "hidden tax" on investment and intermediate inputs will be entirely passed on to consumers, the total CPI-effect of VAT may be in the range of 1 (Zumstein) to 1¼ per cent (KOF) in 1995.

Eventually, labour unions could try to recuperate VAT-induced real income losses and trigger a wage-price spiral. However, the tightness of monetary conditions and high unemployment will leave little scope for real wage increases in excess of productivity gains in the next wage round in the autumn of 1995.

(continued on next page)

(continued)

Timing

The short-run adjustment of the CPI to VAT also depends on the frequency of price recording for different CPI categories. For example, prices of government services such as transport, energy and communication are recorded primarily in January. On the other hand, prices for overnight stays in hotels are only recorded every November so that their VAT effect will impact on the CPI only by end-1995. Due to the different recording times, the estimated distribution of the above described *direct* effect of 1.7 percentage point is the following: in January 0.6 percentage point, in February 0.8, in March 0.2 and in November 0.1 percentage point.

Figure 8. **LABOUR COST AND PRODUCTIVITY**

Percentage change

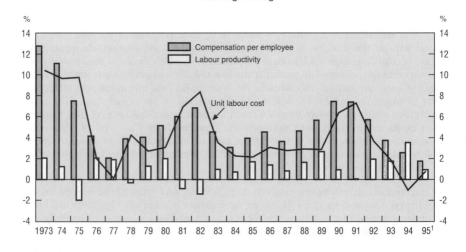

1. Projection.
Source: OECD.

24

VAT-induced price effect has not been incorporated in wage contracts for 1995, which allays worries about a price-wage spiral. However, it also implies that real wages are set to decline in 1995.

Robust exports and soaring imports

The economic recovery in the OECD area in 1994, especially in European Member countries, brought about a vigorous upswing in Switzerland's export markets, from a small contraction in 1993 to an expansion by at least 10 per cent in 1994. However, the appreciation of the Swiss franc which had begun in 1992 accelerated in 1994, so that in nominal effective (trade-weighted) terms the average exchange rate was about 10 per cent higher in 1994 than in 1992. In real effective terms the appreciation was equally substantial: expressed in relation either to relative export prices or to relative unit labour cost in common currency, the real Swiss franc exchange rate has also risen by nearly 11 per cent from 1992 to 1994 (Figure 9). Hence, although merchandise export volumes grew by a brisk 5 per cent in 1994, following a weak 0.6 per cent in 1993, this meant a sizeable loss in market share. Moreover, the 1994 export performance was accomplished at the expense of price concessions made by exporters, which are likely to have exceeded the reduction in unit labour costs. Profit margins of exporters are estimated to have shrunk in 1994, for the fifth year in a row.

Growth of merchandise export volumes was particularly buoyant in the second half of 1994, after a disappointing second quarter. They weakened mark-edly – on a seasonally-adjusted basis – in the first quarter of 1995, probably reflecting the loss in price competitiveness ensuing from the Swiss franc appreci-ation. Benefiting from accelerating industrial production and restocking in many OECD countries, raw materials and semi-finished goods proved the most buoyant export category in 1994, rising by more than 9 per cent in volume terms (Table 5), though some weakening has been recorded towards the end of 1994 and in the first quarter of 1995. Export volumes of investment goods, which had been sluggish in the first half of 1994, took the lead thereafter and accelerated to a s.a.a.r. of 14 per cent in the second half; they stabilised at this high level in the first quarter of 1995. The annual growth of real investment goods exports of 5½ per cent in 1994 was slightly faster than the growth of private non-residential investment in the OECD area. It compares particularly favourably with the

Figure 9. **COMPETITIVENESS AND TRADE**[1]

Index 1987 = 100

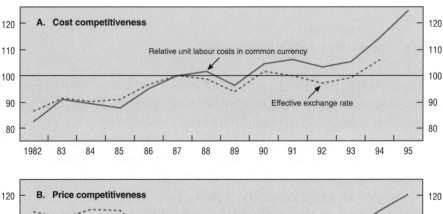

A. Cost competitiveness

Relative unit labour costs in common currency

Effective exchange rate

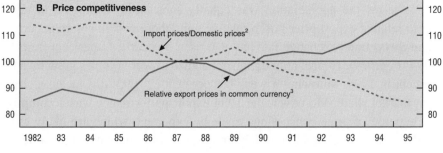

B. Price competitiveness

Import prices/Domestic prices[2]

Relative export prices in common currency[3]

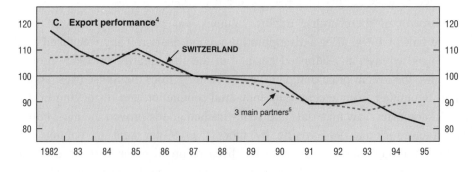

C. Export performance[4]

SWITZERLAND

3 main partners[5]

1. 1995 figures are Secretariat projections.
2. Import prices of total goods and services divided by deflator of total domestic demand.
3. Manufactures.
4. Ratio between export volumes of manufactures and export markets for manufactures.
5. Germany, France and Italy.
Source: OECD.

Table 5. Foreign trade by commodity group[1]

| | 1992 values | | | | Percentage change from previous period, annual rates, s.a. | | | | | | | | | |
| | SF million | % share | 1993 | 1994 | 1993 | | | | 1994 | | | | 1995 |
					Q1	Q2	Q3	Q4	Q1	Q2	Q3	Q4	Q1
Imports, cif, total													
Volume	86 739	100.0	-1.3	9.4	-7.5	7.3	8.7	12.5	8.6	8.2	9.0	11.6	16.0
Price			-2.2	-4.8	4.6	-4.4	-1.8	-6.5	-12.4	-0.2	0.4	2.5	-9.3
Raw materials													
and semi-finished goods													
Volume	26 800	30.9	-1.3	10.9	-9.8	10.9	5.4	6.3	19.3	2.1	17.9	18.1	-5.3
Price			-2.7	-3.9	2.9	-3.8	-4.9	-4.5	-9.9	-0.5	0.7	5.3	4.7
Fuels													
Volume	3 898	4.5	-8.5	2.9	16.5	-30.8	-0.7	47.5	-7.2	16.5	-32.4	37.8	-29.5
Price			-3.5	-14.0	32.5	-5.3	-20.2	-23.5	-20.2	-1.6	3.4	-19.3	-2.3
Investment goods													
Volume	22 449	25.9	-4.1	13.6	-6.3	-2.4	13.9	24.7	7.0	7.2	35.1	-0.5	95.8
Price			-1.5	-7.2	4.8	0.1	-4.1	-9.1	-14.9	-1.9	-3.3	1.8	-8.8
Consumer goods													
Volume	33 593	38.7	1.5	6.4	-6.8	12.5	13.4	3.5	8.0	7.1	-2.1	7.9	4.2
Price			-2.1	-3.0	4.1	-7.0	2.8	-3.0	-12.9	3.1	0.2	5.2	-21.8
Exports, fob, total													
Volume	86 148	100.0	0.6	4.9	2.7	5.5	6.6	5.5	4.7	-10.3	22.5	16.1	-6.4
Price			0.0	-0.7	-3.1	3.0	-1.4	0.4	-0.8	-0.8	2.7	-2.3	-6.9
Raw materials													
and semi-finished goods													
Volume	25 654	29.8	-1.7	9.4	-7.6	2.6	16.8	0.7	21.0	-2.5	16.0	9.1	-7.1
Price			-0.7	-3.3	1.8	-0.6	-6.8	-1.9	-8.2	0.9	-1.9	2.3	6.4
Investment goods													
Volume	31 108	36.1	-2.2	5.6	-5.5	12.6	7.0	4.7	2.3	-5.6	19.7	22.6	-1.0
Price			-1.1	-1.2	-2.9	-4.3	-0.6	-5.5	6.2	-5.9	-2.3	-0.8	-3.7
Consumer goods													
Volume	29 294	34.0	5.6	0.7	21.2	2.2	-2.8	9.4	-3.7	-19.4	29.9	14.7	-9.3
Price			1.6	1.9	-3.1	11.3	3.8	5.2	3.8	0.0	-2.8	-10.2	-15.9

1. Index II: excluding precious metals, precious stones, works of art and antiques.
Source: KOF/ETH, *Konjunktur.*

1¾ per cent growth of this demand category in European OECD countries and with the fall in machinery and equipment investment in Germany in 1994, Switzerland's most important trading partner country, which absorbs about one-quarter of Swiss merchandise exports. On the other hand, exports of consumption goods, which had been a major engine of domestic activity in 1993, broadly stagnated in real terms, falling behind household consumption growth in the OECD as well as in European countries. Consumer goods exports (s.a.) fell by an annual rate of 9¼ per cent in the first quarter of 1995.

Due to the fall in export prices, nominal exports (in Swiss franc terms) only expanded by 4.1 per cent in 1994. Exports to European destinations grew in importance in the second half of the year (Figure 10), in line with recovering investment in the European Union. Sales (in current prices) to Germany and France grew by more than 5 per cent in 1994, but exports to Italy, the third biggest single country market, fell slightly, in spite of rising domestic demand, which is likely to be the effect of the depreciation of the lira against the Swiss franc by about 25 per cent during 1993/94. Demand for Swiss goods was strong in non-European OECD countries in 1994, in particular in the United States (+6½ per cent), Japan (+10¾ per cent) and Australia (+11½ per cent). Exports to non-OECD countries, which were a mainstay of demand in 1993, slowed during 1994, mainly on account of falling exports to OPEC countries and to China. But exports to European non-OECD countries and to the Newly Independent states of the former Soviet Union remained very strong.

After three years of decline in nominal as well as in real terms, imports recovered vigorously in 1994 and in the first quarter of 1995. The growth of import volumes by 9.4 per cent in 1994 was mainly due to the sharp turnaround in imported investment goods – which advanced by 13½ per cent – and the surge by nearly 11 per cent of raw material and semi-finished goods import volumes, which had been induced by the strong expansion of industrial production and inventory accumulation. The 6½ per cent volume increase in consumer goods imports in 1994 is remarkable against the background of sluggish household spending in Switzerland. In part, brisk consumer goods imports are likely to be a result of a backlog of demand built up during three years of recession. However, another major source of import buoyancy has been the substantial fall in the prices of all major merchandise import categories in both 1993 and 1994, due to the marked appreciation of the Swiss franc, which appears to have given rise in

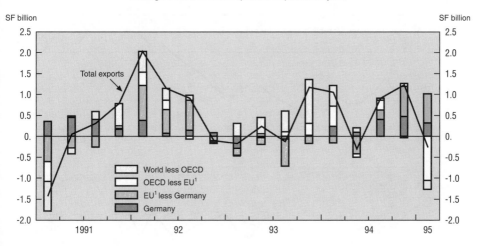

Figure 10. **REGIONAL DISAGGREGATION OF CHANGES IN EXPORTS**
Change over the same quarter of previous year

1. Fifteen Member countries.
Source: OECD, *Monthly Statistics of Foreign Trade.*

numerous cases to the substitution of Swiss made goods by imported products. Altogether, the steeper fall in import prices (–4.8 per cent) than in export prices (–0.7 per cent) in 1994, helped to keep the fob-cif trade account in surplus; this being SF 3.0 billion or some ³/₄ per cent of GDP in 1994 (Figure 11). It was the second consecutive trade surplus after a period of persistent deficits from 1977 to 1992. However, the (s.a.) improvement in the terms of trade was more than offset by the deterioration in real net exports in the first quarter of 1995, so that the trade balance posted an annualised deficit of SF 924 million.

In contrast to merchandise trade, services exports stagnated in 1994 on average (–0.2 per cent in real and 0.5 per cent in nominal terms), as a good first quarter was followed by decreases throughout the remainder of the year; a further substantial fall was recorded in the first quarter of 1995. A major factor was the disappointing performance of the tourism sector, which accounts for more than 40 per cent of service exports and which is usually rather price elastic, hence sensitive to exchange rate changes. Tourism revenues in the summer season of 1994 shrank for the fourth year in a row and remained below their average of

Figure 11. **FOREIGN TRADE INDICATORS**

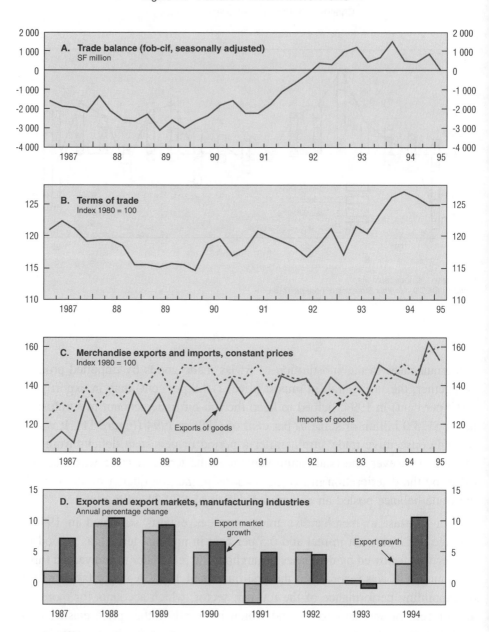

A. Trade balance (fob-cif, seasonally adjusted)
SF million

B. Terms of trade
Index 1980 = 100

C. Merchandise exports and imports, constant prices
Index 1980 = 100

Exports of goods

Imports of goods

D. Exports and export markets, manufacturing industries
Annual percentage change

Export market growth

Export growth

Source: OECD.

30

the past 10 years; this downward trend continued in the first quarter of 1995. Other services components, such as bank commissions, which had been a mainstay of services exports in 1993, also remained rather weak. Services imports were only slightly more buoyant in volume terms, but contracted somewhat in current prices so that the surplus in the non-factor services account barely changed in 1994 (Table 6). With net investment income declining (due to exchange rate appreciation), but the deficit in labour incomes also shrinking somewhat, the surplus in factor incomes decreased and the current external surplus fell from some 8 per cent of GDP in in 1993 to 7 per cent in 1994.[29] Consequent upon the high current external surplus, the ratio of net foreign assets to GDP rose from 105¾ per cent in 1993 to an estimated 107 per cent in 1994, which is by far the highest net foreign asset to GDP ratio in the world.

Table 6. **Balance of payments**

$ billion

	1992	1993	1994	1993		1994	
				I	II	I	II
Seasonally adjusted[1]							
Exports (fob)	67.8	65.4	72.9	32.4	33.0	34.0	38.9
Imports (fob)	65.1	60.3	67.4	29.7	30.6	31.3	36.1
Trade balance	2.7	5.1	5.5	2.8	2.4	2.7	2.8
Services	15.3	16.0	15.9	7.9	8.2	7.4	8.5
Private transfers, net	−2.4	−2.2	−2.6	−1.0	−1.2	−1.3	−1.4
Official transfers, net	−0.6	−0.6	−0.6	−0.3	−0.3	−0.3	−0.4
Current balance	15.1	18.3	18.1	10.2	8.1	9.6	8.5
Not seasonally adjusted							
Current balance	15.1	18.3	18.1				
Non-monetary capital	−6.0	−18.1					
Balance on non-monetary transactions	9.1	0.2					
Short-term monetary capital	−4.6	0.2					
Balance on official settlements	4.4	0.4					
Memorandum items (SF billion):							
Tourism	2.6	2.2	2.5				
Capital movements	−15.0	−26.4					
Non-monetary capital	−8.5	−26.7					
Bank capital	−6.5	0.3					
Balance on official settlements	6.2	0.6					
Trade balance[2]	−1.0	2.9	2.7				
Current balance	21.2	27.0	24.8				

1. Seasonal adjustment by the OECD. 1993 and 1994 figures are still preliminary.
2. Exports (fob) minus imports (cif).
Source: Banque nationale suisse, *Bulletin mensuel;* OECD.

The outlook to 1996

Current indicators

With the salient exception of declining order inflows in the construction industry in the fourth quarter of 1994, most short-term cyclical indicators pointed to a smooth continuation of the recovery of the Swiss economy at the beginning of 1995. But in the course of the first quarter consumer confidence deteriorated and the recovery in capacity utilisation in industry seems to have stalled (Figure 12). Moreover, a number of business survey indicators such as production prospects, the trend of orders and the business climate no longer appear to be on a clear upward trend, which is likely to be related to the recent strong appreciation of the Swiss franc. Although consumer confidence improved in the second quarter of 1995, the balance of current indicators points to a moderate slowdown in economic growth in 1995.

Policy assumptions

The projections discussed below have been made on the technical assumption of nominal exchange rates remaining unchanged at their levels of 2 May 1995. Consequent upon its substantial recent appreciation, this implies that the value of the Swiss franc in nominal effective terms is $7\frac{1}{2}$ per cent higher in 1995 than in 1994. The National Bank expects money supply growth to accelerate in 1995 but even so base money will probably stay distinctly below the envisaged new target trajectory. The decrease in the three-month Euro-Swiss franc interest rate by roughly 1 percentage point to about 3 per cent during the first six months of 1995 and the SNB's cut in the discount rate by $\frac{1}{2}$ percentage point to 3 per cent in late March are consistent with encouraging more rapid money growth. A gradual tightening may be expected for 1996, when economic growth is projected to re-accelerate and headline inflation to stay above the National Bank's medium-term objective of 1 per cent. This could also induce a slight upward drift in long-term interest rates. Following better-than-expected government finances in 1994, further improvements in the general government deficit-to-GDP ratio are unlikely before 1996. This is in part due to the projected slowing of activity this year, but also because government accounts in 1994 were affected by special factors such as postponed expenditures for infrastructure projects, which are bound to entail higher expenditures in 1995.

Figure 12. **INDICATORS OF ACTIVITY**

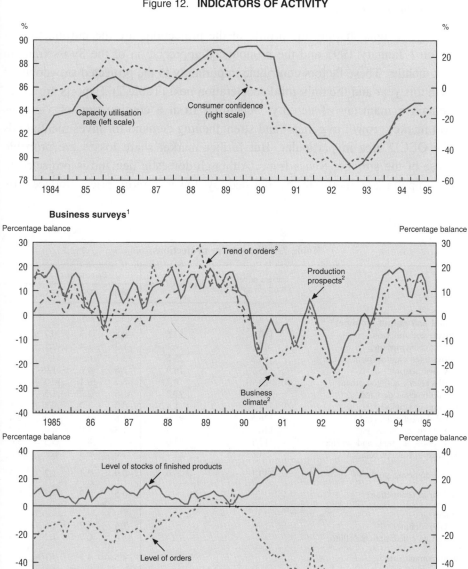

Business surveys[1]

1. Balance of positive and negative orders.
2. 3-month moving average.
Source: KOF/ETH, *Konjunktur,* and OECD, *Main Economic Indicators.*

33

Short-term prospects

Major events shaping the profile of the projections are the introduction of VAT on 1 January 1995 and the pronounced appreciation of the Swiss franc in recent months. These factors contribute importantly to the projected slowdown of growth this year and the only mild acceleration next (Table 7). Exports are likely to remain a mainstay of activity, benefiting from a continuation of vigorous export market growth in general and strengthening demand for investment goods in the OECD area in particular. But further market share losses are probable because of the stronger Swiss franc. Although domestic demand is projected to slow, imports are likely to be boosted by lower import prices induced by

Table 7. **Short-term projections**

	Current prices SF billion 1991	Share in GDP %	Percentage changes			
			1993	1994	1995[1]	1996[1]
Demand and output (volume)[2]						
Private consumption	190.5	57.5	−0.8	1.3	0.7	1.5
Public consumption	46.6	14.1	−1.7	1.4	−0.5	−0.4
Gross fixed capital formation	84.8	25.6	−3.1	6.5	4.2	3.9
Construction	55.9	16.9	−2.8	4.6	1.0	2.0
Machinery and equipment	28.9	8.7	−3.7	10.1	10.0	7.0
Final domestic demand	321.9	97.2	−1.5	2.7	1.5	1.9
Change in stocks[3, 4]	4.5	1.4	−0.3	1.7	0.8	0.5
Total domestic demand	326.5	98.6	−1.8	4.4	2.3	2.4
Exports of goods and services	116.7	35.3	1.3	3.9	4.4	5.0
Imports of goods and services	112.1	33.9	−1.0	8.8	5.5	5.0
Change in foreign balance[3]	4.6	1.4	1.0	−2.3	−0.7	−0.2
Gross domestic product	333.1	100.0	−0.9	2.1	1.7	2.3
Industrial production			−0.5	7.9	4.5	5.0
Prices						
GDP deflator			2.1	1.7	1.6	2.0
Private consumption deflator			3.0	0.7	1.7	1.9
Unemployment rate			4.5	4.7	4.1	3.6
Current balance ($ billion)			18.3	18.1	20.9	21.5
Per cent of GDP			7.9	6.9	7.0	6.8

1. OECD forecast.
2. At 1980 prices.
3. As a percentage of previous year's GDP.
4. Including statistical adjustments.
Source: Swiss national accounts; OECD.

exchange rate appreciation. This is consistent with evidence that exports, but also goods produced for the domestic market, embody an increasing share of imported inputs from Swiss companies producing abroad (outsourcing). Machinery and equipment investment should continue to expand briskly because the back-log of demand has not yet been entirely eliminated, and because the abolition of the turnover tax ("taxe occulte") on investment has increased the profitability of investment. However, leading indicators suggest that construction investment is likely to weaken this year, partly due to the phasing out of the federal investment bonus programme. But some pick up in building activity should be possible in 1996, when household incomes improve and business capacity utilisation increases further. Little support to demand can be expected from household consumption before 1996 as private disposable incomes are likely to be weak in 1995 as a result of wage moderation and increased social security contributions. Government spending is set to remain constrained by ongoing efforts to reduce budget deficits. With terms of trade projected to be broadly unchanged, and the deteriorating real foreign balance projected to be largely offset by further improvements in net investment income, the current external surplus may stay at around 7 per cent of GDP in both 1995 and 1996.

The increase in inflation projected in 1995 is mainly an effect of the replacement of the turnover tax on goods by a general VAT. Owing to the recent exchange rate appreciation, a still substantial output gap and subdued wage growth, it is likely that the actual effect of VAT on the price level will remain below its "mechanical" impact. Given the technical assumption of a constant nominal exchange rate over the projection period, VAT-adjusted inflation may pick up somewhat when the effect of the recent Swiss franc appreciation peters out and the output gap narrows a little. But with the VAT effect falling out of the calculation, measured inflation will probably rise only slightly in 1996, in spite of slightly higher wage increases.

There appear to be two downside risks: first, the household savings ratio could rebound towards earlier higher levels instead of the continuing small fall implicit in the projected modest growth in private consumption in 1995; and second, the large appreciation of the Swiss franc until March 1995 could entail weaker export and stronger import volumes than allowed for in the projections.

II. Economic policy

Monetary policy

Cautious easing of monetary policy

Since the summer of 1992, the Swiss National Bank (SNB) has steadily eased its very tight monetary policy stance, allowing nominal short- and long-term interest rates to decline, economic activity to recover and broad monetary aggregates to expand. However, the very weak growth of the adjusted monetary base during 1994 and in the first half of 1995, the slowdown of the growth of broader monetary aggregates such as M1, and high real short- and long-term interest rates for an early phase of an upswing suggest that monetary conditions are still relatively tight at the current juncture. The marked appreciation of the nominal and real effective Swiss franc exchange rate contributed to a tightening of monetary conditions, which is likely to hold back the full utilisation of human and physical resources. Measures of the output gap suggest that the economy could grow faster without risking accelerating inflation.

Monetary targets and actual developments

In outlining the monetary policy intentions for 1994, the National Bank explicitly ruled out bringing the seasonally-adjusted monetary base[30] (SAMB) fully into line with its medium-term target on the ground that this would require monetary relaxation to a degree which the Bank thought would risk a reacceleration of inflation. The SNB projected the SAMB growth during 1994 to be more than 1 per cent but a little less than 2³/₄ per cent recorded for 1993.[31] This meant that the Bank expected the level of base money to approach its medium-term target path.

36

In the first quarter of 1994, base money growth was indeed relatively strong (4 per cent, s.a.a.r.) but slowed thereafter (Figure 13). Base money even contracted slightly during the second half of the year and remained broadly stagnant in the first half of 1995. Both components of the SAMB contributed to the deceleration of base money during 1994 and the first half of 1995: after a buoyant first quarter, bank deposits held with the SNB fell sharply during the remainder of 1994 and the first half of 1995, to levels below the average of 1993. In addition, (s.a.) notes in circulation, presently accounting for 91 per cent of the SAMB, slowed the pace of their expansion in the second and third quarter of 1994 and decreased slightly in the fourth quarter. Currency demand appears to have recovered in early 1995 but weakened thereafter. Altogether, at 0.6 per cent the growth of the SAMB through 1994 was weaker than the Bank had expected.

Broader monetary aggregates

Rapidly falling short-term interest rates induced money holders to move funds out of time deposits into sight and savings deposits during 1993. This process continued into the first quarter of 1994, when both (s.a.) M1 and M3 (1985 definitions) grew at two-digit annual rates (Table 8). Thereafter, the reshuffling of portfolios appears to have come to an end as M1 and M3 broadly stagnated from the second to the fourth quarter of 1994. In particular the deceleration of M1 in the fourth quarter of 1994 is consistent with weakening economic activity. Growth of broader monetary aggregates (1995 definitions) remained slow during the first five months of 1995.

Short-term interest and exchange rates

If measured by short-term interest rate movements, the process of monetary easing had already begun in early 1990. It stalled in the first half of 1992, when the negative Swiss franc-Deutschemark short-term interest rate differential widened to an extent that the Swiss franc effective (trade-weighted) exchange rate weakened and concerns grew about higher import price inflation. The subsequent monetary tightening pushed the three-month Euro-Swiss franc interest rate up to a new high of 9¼ per cent by mid-1992. The concomitant narrowing of the Swiss-German money market interest rate differential allowed a resumption of the process of monetary relaxation. From mid-1992 on, and notwithstanding further temporary effective Swiss franc depreciation in late 1992 and in the first quarter of 1993, the three-month Euro-Swiss franc interest rate declined rather

Figure 13. **THE ADJUSTED MONETARY BASE**

Seasonally adjusted

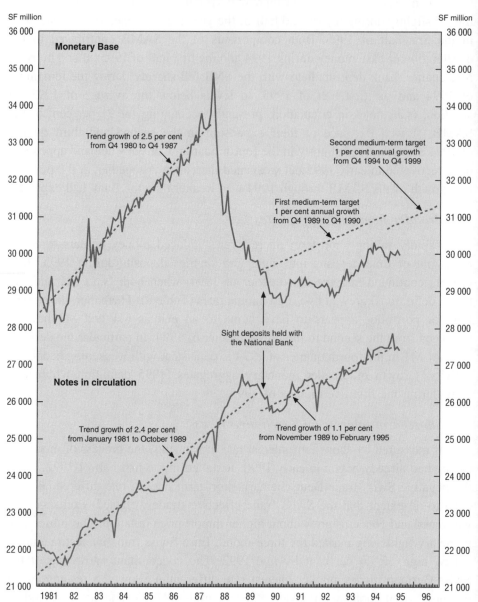

SF million

SF million

Monetary Base

Trend growth of 2.5 per cent
from Q4 1980 to Q4 1987

Second medium-term target
1 per cent annual growth
from Q4 1994 to Q4 1999

First medium-term target
1 per cent annual growth
from Q4 1989 to Q4 1990

Sight deposits held with
the National Bank

Notes in circulation

Trend growth of 2.4 per cent
from January 1981 to October 1989

Trend growth of 1.1 per cent
from November 1989 to February 1995

Source: Banque nationale suisse, *Bulletin mensuel.*

38

Table 8. Monetary aggregates

Percentage change from previous period, s.a.a.r.

	1989	1990	1991	1992	1993	1994	1994 Q2	1994 Q3	1994 Q4	1995 Q1	1995 Q2
Notes in circulation	2.4	-2.1	2.2	0.1	1.5	1.9	1.0	2.2	-0.3	2.5	-2.5
Sight deposits held with SNB	-38.5	-13.5	-6.2	-9.9	3.9	1.0	-3.2	-13.1	-7.1	-11.5	6.0
Adjusted monetary base (AMB)[1]	-5.1	-3.3	1.1	-0.7	1.5	1.9	1.6	0.2	-3.5	1.4	0.6
Sight deposits and transactions accounts	-5.7	-5.9	1.8	2.5	12.9	6.6	-0.3	4.0	0.5	3.0	22.3[2]
M1 (1995 definition)	-4.1	-5.1	1.9	2.0	10.5	5.6	-0.4	3.9	1.2	2.2	16.7[2]
Savings deposits	-7.1	-10.6	1.4	3.6	21.5	13.6	5.3	5.4	1.6	-5.4	11.3[2]
M2 (1995 definition)	-5.7	-8.0	1.7	2.8	16.1	9.9	2.7	4.8	1.4	-2.0	13.7[2]
Time deposits	50.9	26.0	4.4	0.9	-17.4	-7.6	-0.2	-12.3	5.3	15.0	-9.9[2]
M3 (1995 definition)	5.9	2.0	2.7	2.1	4.0	4.9	2.0	0.2	2.4	2.0	7.1[2]
Domestic credit expansion	14.5	11.8	6.7	4.4	1.3	1.7	2.3	2.7	2.0	2.6	–
Nominal GDP	8.2	8.1	5.4	2.3	1.3	3.8	5.7	2.2	2.8	3.3	–
M1 (1985 definition)	-5.5	-4.2	1.2	-0.1	9.3	5.8	-3.3	2.8	0.2	2.0	–
M2 (1985 definition)	20.1	13.0	3.2	0.5	-7.9	-1.9	-1.3	-4.4	3.4	5.9	–
M3 (1985 definition)	6.2	2.4	3.2	2.8	4.8	5.6	1.3	1.0	3.2	3.0	–

1. Change in definition in 1989 and in 1995.
2. Average of April and May annual growth rates.
Source: Banque nationale suisse, *Bulletin mensuel*; OECD.

steadily by more than five percentage points to just above 4 per cent at the end of 1993 (Figure 14).

Throughout 1994 and until January 1995, the three-month Euro-franc interest rate remained broadly stable, hovering around the 4 per cent mark. It came down thereafter, to about 3 per cent in June 1995. In March, the SNB demonstrated its willingness to let short-term rates decline further, when it reduced the discount rate by $\frac{1}{2}$ percentage point to 3 per cent, joining official interest rate cuts in Germany and other European OECD countries. The SNB again lowered the discount rate to $2\frac{1}{2}$ per cent in July 1995. The actions on the discount rate have conveyed signals of monetary ease to markets, although they do not offer any direct relief to banks' refinancing costs as the SNB no longer discounts bills. The flexible Lombard rate remained set at 2 percentage points above the call money rate. It accordingly declined rather steadily from about $6\frac{1}{2}$ per cent at the end of 1993 to around 5 per cent in June 1995.

Judged by the current high level of the real effective Swiss franc exchange rate, monetary conditions appear much tighter than nominal short-term interest rates would suggest (Figure 15). In February 1993, the Swiss franc effective exchange rate was at a temporary trough, which coincided with a very high negative three-month Euro-Swiss franc-Deutschemark interest rate differential of some 3 percentage points. This differential narrowed from then on and the Swiss franc began to appreciate in effective terms. After a short-lived interruption in the winter of 1994/95, the Swiss franc appreciated sharply in March and April 1995 and remained at a high rate in May and June. This unexpected massive increase occurred in the context of international currency turbulences that hit the US dollar and several European currencies. If compared with the annual average of 1992, when the Swiss franc was relatively weak, the effective appreciation until the first half of 1995 amounted to about 16 per cent in nominal terms and some 14 per cent in real[32] terms. In 1994, the Swiss franc appreciated against nearly all major currencies, except the Yen. The appreciation against the Deutschemark from the low level of early 1993 is also substantial: until October 1994 the Swiss franc rose some 11 per cent in nominal terms and a still substantial 8 per cent in inflation-adjusted terms. Owing to the mild upward drift in Deutschemark money market interest rates in late 1994 and slightly declining Swiss franc rates in early 1995, the negative short-term Swiss franc-Deutschemark interest differential widened somewhat, which induced some

Figure 14. **INTEREST RATES**

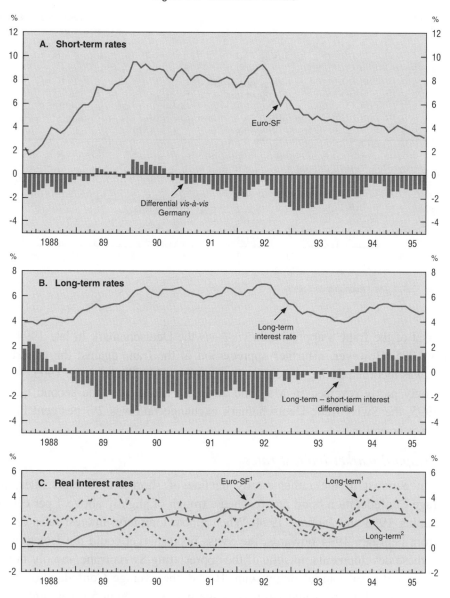

1. Nominal rate less the change in the consumer price index from the previous year.
2. Nominal rate less low frequency component of the annualised change in the s.a. GDP deflator using a Hodrick-
    Prescott filter.
Source: OECD, *Main Economic Indicators,* and estimates.

41

Figure 15. **EXCHANGE RATES**

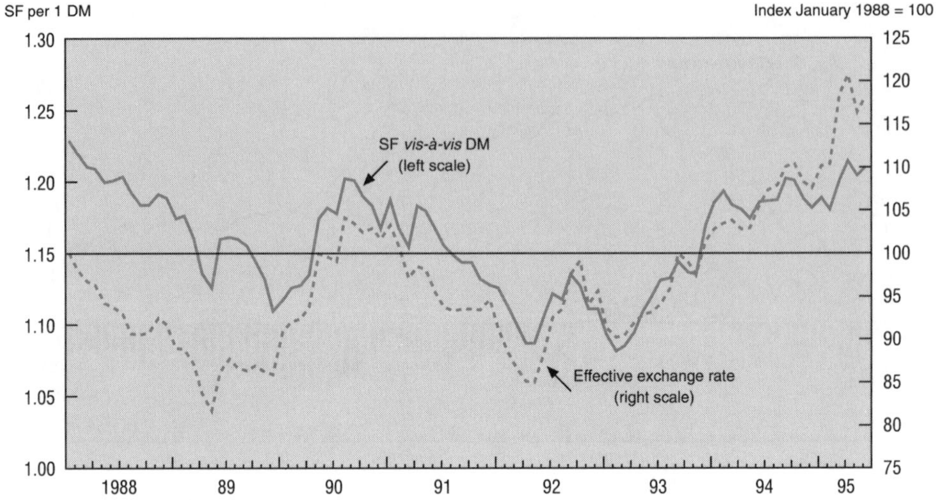

SF per 1 DM

Index January 1988 = 100

Source: OECD, *Main Economic Indicators.*

reversal of the franc's appreciation *vis-à-vis* the Deutschemark in late 1994 and early 1995. However, a further appreciation of the franc against the Deutschemark was recorded during the currency turmoils of March and April 1995, which was only partly reversed in May and June. As a result, in the second quarter of 1995, the Swiss franc-Deutschemark exchange rate was 2¹/₂ per cent higher than a year earlier.

Capital market interest rates

In contrast to the rather steady decline of short-term interest rates, the average Confederation bond rate reached a trough of slightly above 4 per cent in December 1993 and January 1994. When global long-term interest rates drifted up from February 1994 onwards, the Swiss bond market could not isolate itself from these developments, in spite of the appreciating Swiss franc, rapidly falling inflation and a substantial output gap. Hence, the average Confederation bond rate also moved up, by some 1¹/₂ percentage points, reaching 5¹/₂ per cent in the autumn of 1994. It fell back thereafter, to 5¹/₄ per cent by the end of 1994 and further to 4³/₄ per cent in the spring of 1995. The increase during 1994 was smaller than in most other OECD countries (Figure 16) with the notable excep-

42

Figure 16. **INTERNATIONAL COMPARISON OF LONG-TERM INTEREST RATES**
Long-term bond yields[1]

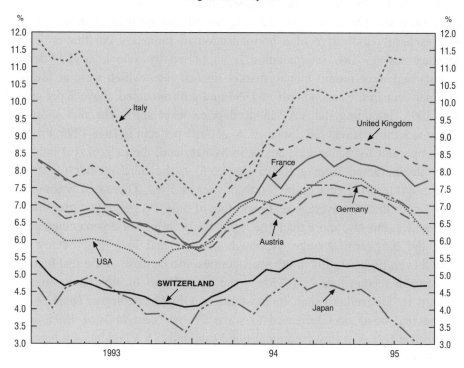

1. Generally ten years.
Source: OECD.

tion of Japan where the rise during 1994 was about ¼ percentage point lower than in Switzerland. The simple econometric model of the Swiss nominal bond rate presented in last year's OECD *Economic Survey of Switzerland* may shed some light on its movements in 1994.[33] A disaggregation of the contributions from the changes in the modelled bond rate suggests that the main factor which contained the rise in Swiss nominal long-term interest rates was the strongly widening negative Swiss-German inflation differential. Some smaller contribution is attributable to the deteriorating Swiss-German growth differential in 1994.

Reflecting the bond rate increase, the slope of the yield curve turned positive at the beginning of 1994, for the first time since the autumn of 1988, reaching a maximum long-short differential of around 1³/₄ percentage points in October 1994. The yield curve flattened thereafter, but maintained a positive slope. With short-term interest rates unchanged, the normalisation of the yield curve is hardly indicative of a normalisation of monetary conditions or even monetary easing. This interpretation is supported by a look at (CPI-deflated *ex post*) real three-month money market interest rates which were at levels of 3-3¹/₂ per cent in the second half of 1994 and still remained above 2 per cent in early 1995, including the VAT-induced price level shift. The real short-term interest rate thus defined fell, however, to about 1 per cent in June 1995. Probably more important for economic activity in Switzerland, the *ex post* real long-term bond rate increased from a low 1 per cent in the third quarter of 1993 to between 4³/₄ to 5 per cent in the fourth quarter of 1994. Thereby it was not only much higher than the average real bond rate of only 1¹/₄ per cent during the past two decades, but also more than one standard deviation (of 2 percentage points) above the long-term average. Although *ex post* real long-term interest rates attained even higher levels in other economies, the increase in the real bond rate between the second half of 1993 and the second half of 1994 was more pro-nounced in Switzerland than in most major OECD countries (Table 9). The *ex post* real bond rate decreased to some 2¹/₂ per cent in June 1995, as the combined effect of a lower nominal bond rate and a VAT-induced jump in the price level.

However, to the extent that inflation expectations of the public are higher than current inflation, *ex ante* real interest rates are lower than those "conven-tionally measured". This appears plausible for Switzerland, where twelve-month CPI-inflation as low as the rate of ¹/₂ per cent recorded in the second half of 1994 has never prevailed for long and is rather unlikely to be preserved once the cyclical upswing gathers more strength. Therefore a somewhat smoother proxy for price expectations appears more plausible. An often used alternative is, for example, modelling inflation expectations as the low frequency component of a Hodrick-Prescott filter applied to the GDP deflator. The real long-term interest rate so defined turns out considerably lower than the conventional concept. Nevertheless, the current level of real interest rates is high for the early phase of an upswing[34] and may – *ceteris paribus* – have a dampening impact on capital expenditure. This also shows that Switzerland is not spared from the current high international level of real interest rates.

Table 9. **Nominal and real interest rates in selected OECD countries**

	1992	1993	1994	1993 Q3	1993 Q4	1994 Q1	1994 Q2	1994 Q3	1994 Q4	1995 Q1	1995 Q2
				Short-term rates [1]							
Nominal rates											
Switzerland	**7.2**	**4.3**	**3.5**	**4.1**	**3.8**	**3.5**	**3.6**	**3.6**	**3.5**	**3.2**	..
United States	3.8	3.3	4.9	3.3	3.4	3.7	4.7	5.2	6.1	6.4	6.0
Germany	9.5	7.3	5.4	6.8	6.4	5.9	5.3	5.0	5.3	5.1	4.6
Japan	4.3	2.9	2.3	3.0	2.2	2.1	2.2	2.3	2.4	2.3	..
United Kingdom	9.6	5.9	5.5	5.9	5.6	5.3	5.2	5.5	6.1	6.7	..
France	10.3	8.6	5.8	7.8	6.7	6.3	5.7	5.6	5.7	6.6	..
				Long-term rates [2]							
Switzerland	**6.4**	**4.6**	**5.0**	**4.4**	**4.1**	**4.3**	**4.9**	**5.3**	**5.3**	**5.2**	**4.7**
United States	8.1	7.2	8.0	6.9	6.8	7.2	7.9	8.2	8.6	8.3	..
Germany	7.9	6.3	6.8	6.2	5.8	6.1	6.7	7.0	7.4	7.2	4.4
Japan	5.3	4.3	4.4	4.2	3.6	4.2	4.1	4.7	4.6	4.2	..
United Kingdom	9.1	7.5	8.2	7.2	6.7	6.8	8.3	8.8	8.7	8.7	..
France	9.0	7.0	7.5	6.7	6.1	6.4	7.4	8.0	8.3	8.1	..
				Short-term							
Inflation-adjusted rates [3]											
Switzerland	**3.2**	**1.0**	**2.7**	**0.7**	**1.2**	**1.8**	**2.9**	**3.1**	**3.0**	**1.8**	..
United States	0.8	0.4	2.3	0.6	0.6	1.2	2.3	2.3	3.5	3.6	2.9
Germany	5.5	3.2	2.3	2.7	2.6	2.5	2.3	2.0	2.5	2.8	2.3
Japan	2.7	1.8	1.7	1.3	1.2	1.0	1.7	2.5	1.8	2.3	..
United Kingdom	5.9	4.4	3.0	4.3	4.0	2.9	2.6	3.2	3.5	3.3	..
France	8.0	6.5	4.2	5.6	4.6	4.6	4.0	4.0	4.1	4.9	..
				Long-term							
Switzerland	**2.4**	**1.3**	**4.1**	**1.0**	**1.5**	**2.7**	**4.3**	**4.7**	**4.9**	**3.8**	..
United States	5.1	4.3	5.4	4.1	4.1	4.6	5.6	5.3	5.9	5.4	..
Germany	3.9	2.2	3.8	2.0	2.1	2.8	3.7	4.0	4.6	4.9	2.1
Japan	3.7	3.1	3.9	2.5	2.6	3.1	3.6	4.9	4.0	4.3	..
United Kingdom	5.3	5.9	5.7	5.6	5.1	4.4	5.8	6.5	6.1	5.3	..
France	6.6	4.9	5.9	4.5	4.0	4.7	5.7	6.3	6.7	6.4	..

1. Domestic rates, mostly for 3 months.
2. Government bond rates, in general.
3. Nominal rates less the annual change in consumer prices.
Source: OECD, *Monthly Financial Statistics* and *Main Economic Indicators.*

Interest rates on new mortgages, which had come down to 5½ per cent at the beginning of 1994, stayed at this level throughout 1994 and until early 1995. Rates on existing mortgages stood at about 6 per cent at the start of 1994 and fell shortly thereafter to 5½ per cent where they remained until February 1995. The decrease in mortgage rates is somewhat surprising as it was in contrast to developments in the bond market. It may reflect intensified competition of banks for shares in a still fragile market for housing loans. The decline in the long- and short-term interest rates during the first half of 1995 has allayed earlier fears of a mortgage-rate increase in the near future.

Monetary policy framework in the medium term

The National Bank's medium-term targeting exercise, which has replaced the earlier annual targeting practice, completed a first five-year period in 1994. In December 1990, the SNB had announced for the first time that it would aim at an expansion of the SAMB by about 1 per cent *per annum* over the medium term, defined as a span of three to five years. The Bank chose as base period of the target path[35] the fourth quarter of 1989, although it was still very uncertain as to whether the commercial banks had fully adjusted their liquidity demand to the regulatory and technical changes that occurred in 1988. The SNB reiterated its adherence to the medium-term target in the following years, although the expansion of the SAMB fell short of the target by a substantial margin right from the first year and stayed below the envisaged target trajectory throughout the chosen period (see Figure 13 above). This was to some extent a consequence of the fact that the target path is interpreted by the SNB as the steady-state expansion of the monetary base, given price stability and output growth in line with its potential. Since even at the end of 1994 there remained an output gap, it was natural that base money was still below the target line.

At the end of 1994, the level of the SAMB was about 3¾ per cent below the medium-term target and its average annual growth from the fourth quarter of 1989 to the fourth quarter of 1994 amounted to only 0.2 per cent (Table 10). The National Bank explains the persistent undershooting of the target during the 1990-94 period in part by the stubbornness of inflation up to 1993 which required greater monetary restriction than planned. This prolonged the recession and depressed base money demand by more than projected. However, the SNB

Table 10. **The 1990-94 base money targeting exercise** [1]

	Target level	Actual level	Deviation from target	Actual growth
	In SF million at fourth quarter		In per cent	
1990	29 866	28 801	–3.6	–2.6
1991	30 164	29 204	–3.2	1.4
1992	30 466	28 925	–5.1	–1.1
1993	30 771	29 724	–3.4	2.8
1994	31 078	29 908	–3.8	0.6
Annual average				0.2

1. The base period of the medium-term target was the fourth quarter of 1989, when the seasonally-adjusted monetary base was at SF 29 570 million.
Source: Banque nationale suisse, *Bulletin mensuel*; OECD.

also concedes that the banks' demand for liquidity was far lower than expected at the time when the first medium-term target was formulated.[36]

Nevertheless, the National Bank concluded that its concept "has stood the test".[37] It therefore decided to repeat the medium-term targeting exercise over the following five years, aiming at an average annual growth of the seasonally-adjusted monetary base of 1 per cent from the fourth quarter of 1994 to the fourth quarter of 1999. This is deemed "adequate to guarantee a stable price level in Switzerland",[38] which the SNB considers to be equivalent to measured consumer price inflation of "roughly 1 per cent".[39] The SNB's assumption of average potential output growth of 2 per cent, its inflation objective and its medium-term monetary target imply a trend increase in the income velocity of base money by 2 per cent per year;[40] the rise in velocity is expected to be a consequence of the growing use of cashless means of payment (*e.g.* credit cards and automated teller machines).

As starting point of the new target path, the SNB chose a SAMB of SF 30 700 million, which is some SF 400 million (1¼ per cent) below the end value of the previous target trajectory (see Figure 15 above). This downward adjustment is the net result of an estimated structural decrease in money demand by SF 700 million (2¼ per cent) during the first medium-term target period,[41] an upward shift by an estimated SF 400 million due to the VAT-induced price-level increase and another downward adjustment by SF 100 million on account of a change in the definition of the monetary base[42] (Table 11). The SNB reckons that starting the new target from the end-point of the first target trajectory would risk

Table 11. **Resetting the medium-term monetary target for the 1995-99 period**

	SF million	Per cent difference from end-value of 1990-94 target path
End-value of 1990-94 target path	31 100	0
Downward shift in base money demand due to improved liquidity management by banks	−700	−2¼
Eliminating non-bank deposits from base money	−100	−¼
Upward shift in base money demand due to VAT	+400	+1¼
Starting-point of 1995-99 target path	30 700	−1¼
Actual value of s.a. monetary base in 1994 Q4	29 908	−3¾

Source: Banque nationale suisse, *Monnaie et conjoncture,* Bulletin trimestriel, December 1994; OECD.

too expansionary a monetary policy stance. The present level of the SAMB being some SF 800 million below the new steady-state target path is, therefore, a consequence of actual output being markedly below its potential at the beginning of 1995 – the SNB estimates an output gap of some 3 per cent. Based on its projection of real output growth slightly above 2 per cent, but a – mainly VAT-induced – price-level increase by 3 per cent on average, the SNB projects growth of base money demand by about 2 per cent in 1995, which it intends to accommodate. Given that from the current perspective the price effect of VAT appears markedly smaller and output growth possibly somewhat lower than originally projected by the SNB, base money demand may again increase by less than expected, which is consistent with the weak growth of SAMB observed in the first half of 1995. This led the SNB to allow money market rates to decline further.

However, in the light of recent movements of the monetary base relative to key macroeconomic magnitudes there are still lingering doubts about whether a stable relationship between the monetary base and nominal GDP really has been re-established. For example, the unexpected decline in the SAMB during the second half of 1994, when money market interest rates remained broadly unchanged, but nominal GDP accelerated, appears in part to be caused by another drop in banks' demand for sight deposits held with the SNB. According to the SNB, however, it is too early to tell if this was a permanent shift. It resulted mainly from a change in the structure of banks' liabilities, reducing the amount of their required liquidity. As to the weak growth of currency demand in the second half of 1994, the SNB ascribes it largely to the unexpectedly rapid decline of the inflation rate. All this may point to another downward shift of the demand for base money, which could result in further undershooting of the National Bank's medium-term target, limiting the base money's value as an anchor for expectations and guide to monetary policy in the short term. In view of possible further instability of demand for base money, other indicators have gained importance in assessing monetary conditions. These indicators include broader monetary aggregates, in particular M1 whose statistical base has been improved recently, the output gap, the exchange rate and wage settlements.

Given that the SNB already makes public which range of measured consumer price inflation it deems consistent with price stability, putting more weight on a broader range of indicators when making monetary policy decisions and announcements would move the Swiss monetary policy approach closer to explicit inflation targeting. Such an approach has been adopted in several countries where structural change in money and credit markets has made the targeting of money supply as well as the interpretation of money demand extremely difficult; examples are New Zealand (since 1990), Canada (since 1991), the United Kingdom (since 1992), and Sweden and Finland (since 1993). Specifics of inflation targeting differ across countries in terms of definition of targets (which price index and which average rate of inflation to be targeted) as well as the range of permissible fluctuations. But in theory, inflation targeting is thought to be most likely to succeed when it is based on an explicit statement on price stability as the *sole* objective of monetary policy and an institutional framework which makes the Central Bank accountable for inflation outcomes. Additional prerequisites are the development of a system of intermediate indicators and tightly focused policy reports, to make clear how the objective with respect to inflation control is made operational.

Improved monetary statistics

Until recently, the indicative value of broader monetary aggregates had been impaired by flaws in the definitions of aggregates.[43] Presumably the most serious shortcoming of the revision of Swiss monetary statistics in 1985 was the exclusion of transaction accounts, in particular salary accounts (*"comptes salaires"*),

Box 2. Overview of the 1995 revisions to monetary statistics[1]

Old definitions (1985)

M1   = currency in circulation in Swiss francs
      + residents' sight deposits in Swiss francs held with banks and the postal giro system

M2   = M1
      + residents' time deposits in Swiss francs

M3   = M2
      + residents' savings deposits (including transaction accounts and "second[2] and third pillar"[3] retirement savings)

New definitions (1995)

M1   = currency in circulation
      + residents' sight deposits in Swiss francs held with banks and the postal giro system
      + transaction accounts (including salary accounts)

M2   = M1
      + savings deposits (excluding those which are already counted as transaction accounts and excluding "second and third pillar" retirement savings accounts)

M3   = M2
      + residents' time deposits in Swiss francs

Differences between old and new definitions

M1 (1995) = M1 (1985)
      + transaction accounts (including salary accounts)

M2 (1995) = M2 (1985)
      + transaction accounts
      + savings deposits (excluding those which are already counted as transaction accounts and excluding "second and third pillar" retirement savings accounts)
      – time deposits

(continued on next page)

(continued)

M3 (1995) = M3 (1985)
- "second and third pillar" retirement savings accounts

---

1. A more detailed account of the revisions is given in "Révision de la statistique monétaire", *Monnaie et conjoncture*. Bulletin trimestriel de la Banque nationale suisse, mars 1995.
2. Occupational insurance via private pension and provident funds.
3. Individual old-age insurance in the form of savings encouraged through tax incentives.

from M1. This made M1 an incomplete indicator of money held for transaction purposes because the omitted accounts are highly liquid and are therefore widely used for payments. Partly because these transaction accounts initially earned interest comparable to those on savings accounts, the SNB had considered them as close substitutes to savings deposits and included them in M3. But since 1988 interest rates on transaction accounts have been substantially below those of savings deposits, making these accounts more similar to sight deposits. Another problem was that the transaction accounts were not recorded by commercial banks in a uniform way; some banks considered them sight deposits and others savings deposits, and recording practices by individual banks varied over the years.

To remedy all this and to make further amendments in order to improve the meaningfulness of monetary aggregates, the SNB embarked on a major redefinition of monetary statistics, with the new definitions coming into effect as from January 1995; the changes are sketched out in Box 2. The main innovations are the inclusion of transaction accounts in M1, which should enable it to capture variations in economic activity better, and the replacement of time deposits by the more liquid (redefined) savings deposits in M2. This makes the conceptual difference biggest for M2, while the modification to M3 is rather minor. A comparison of rates of change of old and new aggregates shows that – with the possible exception of 1992 – trends of M1 in the two definitions were similar in recent years; roughly the same holds for M3. In contrast, the new M2 displayed behaviour diametrically different from that of its old counterpart in 1989-90 and in 1993-94, being now more in line with movements of M1 and M3. Fluri[44] (1995) reports that the income velocity of the new M1 shows a theoretically more plausible pattern than the previous definition as it is better correlated with the bond rate; moreover, he demonstrates that the replacement of the old by the new M1 improves the predictive power of a simple model for inflation based on M1.

Fiscal policy

Overview

For the first time in almost a decade, government finances are estimated to have improved in 1994; the deficit on the consolidated account of the general government including social security fell by 0.5 percentage point to 3.1 per cent of GDP (Table 12).[45] The succession of budget deficits in recent years has increased the combined gross debt of the Confederation, cantons and communes from 32 per cent of GDP in 1990 to an estimated 47 per cent of GDP in 1994 (Figure 17); the latter comprises 21 per cent for the Confederation, 15 per cent for the cantons and 11 per cent for the communes.

The consolidated deficit may decline further in 1995, mainly as result of prospective budgetary improvements at lower levels of government. Allowing for the effects of the consolidation programme approved by Parliament at the beginning of 1995, the Confederation's deficit[46] is projected to decline from SF 6.1 billion in 1995 to about F 4 billion (1 per cent of GDP) in 1998. Half of this reduction is estimated to be structural. Further budgetary consolidation will be required to achieve the Confederation's objective of reducing gross debt as a percentage of GDP in the medium term.

The Confederation's finances in 1994[47]

On a financial accounts basis, the Confederation's deficit fell to SF 5.1 billion (1.4 per cent of GDP) in 1994 from SF 7.8 billion (2.2 per cent of GDP) the year before (Table 13). This improvement reflected both lower growth in expenditures and higher growth in revenues than that of GDP. The principal

Table 12. **Government accounts**

SF million and percentage changes

	1991 SF million	Outturns			Budgets [1]	
		1992	1993	1994 [2]	1994	1995
Confederation [3]						
Expenditure	35 501	6.5	7.4	1.8	7.2	−0.4
Revenue	31 457	4.2	−4.2	10.3	−1.8	2.6
Balance	−4 044	−5 040	−9 199	−6 706	−8 166	−7 051
Cantons						
Expenditure	45 626	5.9	8.4	−	2.6	2.2
Revenue	41 845	5.6	6.4	−	1.1	4.1
Balance	−3 781	−4 159	−5 390	−3 700	−5 000	−4 200
Communes						
Expenditure	33 239	8.2	5.6	−	5.1	1.3
Revenue	31 088	6.9	6.1	−	5.2	2.7
Balance	−2 151	−2 730	−1 750	−1 250	−2 500	−2 000
General government [4]						
Expenditure	96 272	6.9	8.0	−	4.7	0.4
Revenue	86 296	5.5	3.1	−	0.8	2.9
Balance	−9 976	−11 929	−16 339	−11 656	−15 666	−13 251
As a percentage of GDP	−3.0	−3.5	−4.8	−3.3	−4.4	−3.6
Social security						
Expenditure	29 330	15.3	3.5	−	−	−
Revenue	32 247	4.9	12.5	−	−	−
Balance	+2 917	+27	+3 070	+991	−	−
Consolidated account of general government and social security						
Expenditure	116 960	9.0	6.6	−	−	−
Revenue	109 901	5.5	3.1	−	−	−
Balance	−7 059	−11 902	−13 269	−10 665	−	−
As a percentage of GDP	−2.1	−3.5	−3.9	−3.1	−	−

1. Initial budget on initial budget.
2. Budget projections for the cantons and communes and estimates for social security.
3. These accounts have been constructed using the definitions of the "Statistique financière révisée". This makes the Confederation accounts comparable with those of the cantons and communes, making possible the aggregation of the accounts of all three levels of government to obtain estimates for general government finances.
4. Not including social security.
Source: Administration fédérale des finances.

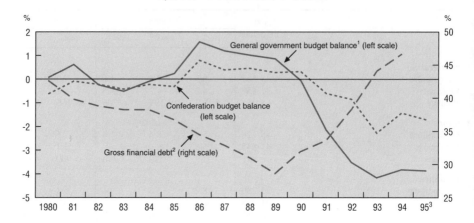

Figure 17. **BUDGET BALANCES AND DEBT**
As per cent of GDP, transactions basis

General government budget balance[1] (left scale)

Confederation budget balance
(left scale)

Gross financial debt[2] (right scale)

1. Including social security.
2. Of the Confederation, cantons and communes.
3. Projection.
Source: Office fédéral des questions conjoncturelles.

factor accounting for the low growth in expenditures was a large reduction in loans to the unemployment insurance fund;[48] without this factor, expenditure would have grown slightly as a proportion of GDP. This reduction was possible because unemployment did not continue to deteriorate in 1994, as had been expected when the 1993 loans were made. With respect to revenues, the high growth in 1994 reflects the effect on even-numbered years of the biennial system for collecting federal income taxes rather than strong underlying growth.[49] Between the more comparable years of 1992 and 1994, revenue only grew at an annual average rate of 1.8 per cent, reflecting the effects of the recession on income growth in 1991-92 (the base period for federal income taxes to be paid in 1994-95). Receipts from indirect taxation have also been subdued, owing to the effects of the declining base for the turnover tax (ICHA) prior to its replacement by the VAT on 1 January 1995.

Compared with the 1994 budget, the deficit outturn was SF 1.9 billion lower than projected, again mainly on account of lower than anticipated loans to the unemployment insurance fund.[50] Transport expenditure was also significantly

Table 13. **Central government budget**[1]

SF million

	1991		1992		1993		1994		Initial budget	Percentage changes[2]		
	Outturns	Breakdown in %	Initial budget	Outturns	Initial budget	Outturns	Initial budget	Outturns		1993	1994	1995
Total expenditure	35 501	100.0	37 117	37 816	39 737	40 600	42 583	41 341	42 399	7.4	1.8	2.6
Economic classification												
Compensation of employees	4 393	12.4	4 547	4 764	4 788	4 748	4 970	4 923	4 938	−0.3	3.7	0.3
Consumption	5 560	15.7	5 689	5 675	5 456	5 359	5 693	5 462	5 711	−5.6	1.9	4.6
Investment	719	2.0	854	810	834	934	849	815	824	15.3	−12.7	1.1
Interest, loans, acquisition of holdings	2 634	7.4	2 784	3 079	4 254	5 033	5 346	4 590	4 096	64.1	−9.2	−10.8
Transfers	22 195	62.5	23 243	23 488	24 405	24 506	25 725	25 551	26 830	4.3	4.3	5.0
Total revenue	33 490	100.0	35 788	34 953	36 651	32 782	35 609	36 239	36 319	−6.2	10.5	0.2
Tax revenue	29 169	87.1	31 886	30 406	32 344	28 589	31 498	31 428	32 053	−6.0	9.9	2.0
Direct taxes	12 888	38.5	14 750	14 269	13 850	11 993	14 150	14 493	13 400	−16.0	20.8	−7.5
Indirect taxes	16 281	48.6	17 136	16 137	18 494	16 596	17 348	16 935	18 653	2.8	2.0	10.1
Other revenue	4 321	12.9	3 902	4 547	4 307	4 193	4 111	4 811	4 266	−7.8	14.7	−11.3
Balance	−2 011		−1 329	−2 863	−3 086	−7 818	−6 974	−5 102	−6 080			
As a percentage of GDP	−0.6		−0.4	−0.8	−0.9	−2.3	−2.0	−1.4	−1.6			

1. Financial account.
2. For 1993 and 1994: outturn on outturn of previous period; for 1995: initial budget on outturn for 1994.

Source: Budget of the Swiss Confederation.

55

lower than projected, at least in part reflecting the freezing of funds voted for highway construction following the referendum vote in favour of the Alpine initiative. Revenue in 1994 was a little higher than projected in the budget, mainly reflecting a larger than projected surplus on the "Caisse fédérale d'Assurances" (CFA)[51] owing to higher than expected interest rates and contributions. Although total tax revenues were in line with budget projections, direct tax was a little higher and indirect tax a little lower than projected.

The 1995 government budgets

The combined deficit of the Confederation, cantons and communes is projected to fall by SF 2.4 billion (0.8 per cent of GDP) from the level budgeted for 1994 to SF 13.3 billion in 1995 (3.6 per cent of GDP) (see Table 12).[52] Of this projected reduction in the budgeted deficit, a little under half is attributable to the Confederation, one third to the cantons and the rest to the communes.

Compared with the level budgeted for 1994, Confederation expenditures are projected to decline by 0.4 per cent in 1995 (Table 14). The main factor contributing to this reduction is, once again, the projected decline in payments to the unemployment insurance fund (AC);[53, 54] abstracting from these payments, expenditure is projected to grow by 3.2 per cent. The decline in these payments reflects both a projected reduction in unemployment and, from 1 January 1995, two discretionary measures to strengthen the unemployment insurance fund's financial position: an increase in the contribution rate from 2 to 3 per cent of earnings; and the introduction of a stand-down period of 5 days before a person who becomes unemployed is eligible for compensation. The otherwise low growth in expenditures is mainly attributable to reductions in expenditure on goods and services, in contributions to investment by lower levels of government (especially road building) and in compensation of employees. With respect to the latter, the reductions are to be achieved mainly by not compensating federal employees for inflation in 1994 and by cutting a further 100 posts.[55] In contrast to the subdued outlook for most categories of expenditures, social welfare other than unemployment compensation is projected to grow strongly.[56] This high growth is mainly attributable to the increased payments to the sickness insurance fund (AM) to reduce premiums (5 per cent of VAT revenues are to be so dedicated) and to the biennial indexation of age and invalidity pensions (AVS/AI). Debt interest payments are also projected to grow strongly, mainly reflecting higher interest rates.

Table 14. **Composition and growth in the Confederation's expenditure, 1995**

Main categories	1995 budget SF million	Percentage share	Change 1995/94 [1]	
			SF million	Percentage change
Total expenditure	42 399	100.0	−184	−0.4
Current expenditure	37 634	88.8	+1 797	+5.0
Personnel	4 938	11.6	−32	−0.6
Goods and services	3 096	7.3	−137	−4.2
Defence	2 615	6.2	+155	+6.3
Debt interest	3 323	7.8	+502	+17.8
Cantonal share of federal revenues	2 916	6.9	−167	−5.4
Indemnities to other government entities	622	1.5	−10	−1.6
Contributions to current expenditure of social security and lower levels of government	20 124	47.5	+1 486	+8.0
Investment	4 765	11.2	−1 981	−29.4
Investment goods	824	1.9	−25	−2.9
Loans and equity	773	1.8	−1 752	−69.4
Contributions to investment of lower levels of government	3 168	7.5	−204	−6.0

1. Initial budget on initial budget.
Source: Administration fédérale des finances.

The Confederation's receipts are projected to grow by 2.0 per cent in 1995 from the level budgeted for 1994, considerably less than the projected growth in (nominal) GDP (Table 15).[57] This low growth reflects the depressing effect of the biennial system for collecting federal income taxes on revenue in odd-numbered years.[58] Tax revenues from sources not affected by this distortion are projected to grow by 6.2 per cent in 1995. Most of this growth is attributable to the replacement of the turnover tax (ICHA) with the VAT, even though VAT revenue will be received for only three quarters in 1995.[59] Large increases are also projected for stamp duties and for tobacco tax. For the taxes affected by the biennial system, a more meaningful comparison is with the budget projections in the previous odd-numbered year, 1993. On this basis, growth is projected to be low for federal income tax receipts but high for receipts from withholding tax. The low growth in federal income tax receipts reflects the recession in the early 1990s (tax payments in 1994-1995 are based on income in 1991-92) and the indexation of tax scales up to the end of 1991. With respect to the withholding tax, the high

Table 15. **Composition and growth in the Confederation's receipts, 1995**

	1995 budget SF million	Percentage of total	Percentage change per annum	
			1995/93 [1]	1995/94 [2]
Total receipts	36 319	100.0	+5.3	+2.0
Tax revenue	32 053	88.3	+5.9	+1.8
Federal income tax	8 650	23.8	+4.7	–4.4
Withholding tax	2 900	8.0	+22.6	–14.7
Stamp duty	1 850	5.1	–7.9	+8.8
Turnover tax/VAT	10 700	29.5	+6.8	+11.5
Tobacco tax	1 360	3.7	+8.0	+11.9
Customs duties	1 196	3.3	+1.3	+0.2
Fuel duties	4 470	12.3	+6.2	+0.4
Other	927	2.6	+0.4	+4.3
Other receipts	4 266	11.7	+0.9	+3.8

1. Initial budget on outcome.
2. Initial budget on initial budget.
Source: Administration fédérale des finances.

growth projected reflects a large decline in refunds for the tax period 1991-92, when interest and dividend earnings were much lower than in the preceding two-year period. These projections underline two structural weaknesses in the Confederation's receipts: the volatility of withholding tax and stamp duties, which together account for 13 per cent of revenues; and the tendency for import duties, which are levied on physical quantities, to fall over time as a proportion of import values.

Growth in cantons' expenditures is projected in the 1995 budgets to slow to 2.2 per cent compared with the 1994 budgets.[60] As for the Confederation, a major factor underpinning this slowing is the projected reduction in loans to the unemployment insurance fund (AC). Abstracting from these loans, expenditures are projected to grow by 4.7 per cent. Growth is to be held to this rate, despite large increases in interest payments on public debt and in transfers, mainly by constraining growth in personnel expenditures, the most important item of expenditure in most cantons. This restraint is to be achieved through a continued reduction in the number of employees in most cantons and by not compensating employees in a number of cantons for inflation.

Weak growth in income tax receipts (3.1 per cent), the cantons' principal source of revenue, and in federal income tax receipts (the cantons' share of which is 30 per cent), is projected to be offset by higher growth in the cantons' other revenue sources. The low growth in income tax receipts reflects the unfavourable economic conditions prevailing during 1993-94, the period for which income tax receipts are being collected in most cantons in 1995 and 1996.

None of the 26 cantons is projected to be able to self-finance its net investment in 1995 and only three (Appenzell Rh.-Int., Glaris, and Grisons) are projected to have a rate of self-financing in excess of 60 per cent, a rate considered to be satisfactory. Indeed, four cantons are projected to have recourse to borrowing even to help fund their current expenditures. Overall, the rate of self-financing of net investment is projected to be 18 per cent, as low as in the budgets for 1994.

Cyclically-adjusted budget balances[61]

The cyclically-adjusted budget balance on the consolidated account of general government fell from a peak of 3 per cent of GDP in 1992 to 1.7 per cent of GDP in 1993, where it is estimated to have remained in the following two years. This decline mainly reflected reductions in the deficits of the cantons. Much of the estimated structural deficit in 1995 is attributable to the Confederation (1.3 per cent of GDP), with the cantons also accounting for a significant (0.7 per cent of GDP), albeit smaller, part of the structural deficit; a small deficit is projected for the communes and a surplus is projected for the social security system. Hence, it is the Confederation and, to a lesser extent, the cantons where discretionary policy measures are still required to eliminate structural budget deficits.

An acute uncertainty surrounding these estimates concerns the "non-accelerating-wage rate of unemployment" (NAWRU). Prior to 1991, the unemployment rate was always below 1.1 per cent and estimates of the NAWRU based on expectations-augmented Phillips curves were around 0.8 per cent. But the subsequent large increase in unemployment relative to the change in output suggests that there has been a significant rise in the NAWRU. The estimates of cyclically-adjusted-budget balances presented here assume that the NAWRU rose progressively from 0.8 per cent in 1990 to 2.5 per cent in 1994 and subsequently remained at this level.

The 1994 consolidation programme[62]

The 1994 consolidation programme is the third in recent years. The previous two, in 1992 and 1993, are estimated to have reduced structural deficits in the medium term by around SF 7 billion. Consolidation in the first two programmes gave equal weight to cutting expenditures and to increasing revenues.[63] Despite the first and second consolidation programmes being on track to achieve their objectives, the structural deficit projected in 1998 was still estimated to be about SF 4 billion (1.0 per cent of GDP); the unadjusted deficit in 1998 was projected to be more than SF 6 billion. The objective of the 1994 consolidation programme proposed by the Federal Council was to eliminate this remaining structural deficit.

Approximately half of the reduction in the deficit proposed in the 1994 consolidation programme was to be achieved through lower expenditure growth (Table 16). About a quarter of these economies related to measures requiring changes in the law. These measures are mostly related to the social welfare system, notably reductions in the Confederation's share of contributions to the old age insurance fund (AVS); an increase in the self-employed workers' contribution rates for old-age insurance (AVS), invalidity insurance (AI) and loss-of-earnings insurance (APG) to the same levels as those for employees; and the indexation of age and invalidity pensions to prices instead of the average of prices and wages. It was also proposed to reduce subsidies for highway maintenance, abandon refunds of fuel taxes to the groups concerned (mainly farmers and providers of concessional public transport) and to extend the linear cuts in subsidies until 1997. The major economies proposed in terms of the data of the financial plan concerned reductions in the budgets for national defence, highway construction, foreign affairs (notably, development aid) and general administration. With respect to revenues, which were projected to rise by SF 1½ billion compared with the baseline by 1998, the main increases were from petrol and fuel taxes (a little over SF 1 billion per year), a move to a proportional company income tax rate with the rate set at the present maximum (9.8 per cent, increasing tax receipts by SF 560 million for the tax period 1995-96) and a change in the basis for calculating cigarette tax, yielding an extra SF 70 million per year.

The Federal Council also indicated that it is pursuing a number of structural reforms which are likely to reduce structural deficits in the long-term but which are not quantified. These include a critical review of federal subsidies (report due

Table 16.   **The 1994 consolidation programme of the Confederation**

SF million

	1995	1996	1997	1998
Budgetary improvements				
Proposed by the Federal Council				
Measures requiring constitutional change		24	40	40
Measures requiring legislation	56	286	451	453
Extension of linear cuts in subsidies		250	250	
Total	56	560	741	493
Measures by decree	35	83	217	217
Financial plan targets	1 199	1 243	1 385	1 318
Total savings	1 290	1 886	2 343	2 028
Extra receipts		1 120	1 335	1 545
Improvement in primary budget balance	1 290	3 006	3 678	3 573
Reduction in debt interest payments from lower deficits		130	280	450
Improvement in budget balance	1 290	3 136	3 958	4 023
Accepted by Parliament				
Total savings	1 290	1 931	2 209	1 862
Extra receipts	–	75	75	75
Improvement in primary budget balance	1 290	2 006	2 284	1 937

Source: Federal Council of Switzerland, *Message sur les mesures d'assainissement des finances fédérales 1994.*

this year), relaxation of norms and standards judged to be excessive for public works (report published in 1995), reform of the federal administration (report due in 1995), the imposition of constitutional limits on federal deficits and debt and reform of financial relations with the cantons (report due in 1996). With respect to the reform of federal administration, the major objectives are to eliminate the doubling-up of tasks, to improve co-ordination and coherence, to take advantage of synergies and to attribute tasks and responsibilities clearly. In the case of the constitutional limit on deficits and debt, the aim is to impose a requirement that any structural deficits must be countered by corrective measures which eliminate them. The reform of financial relations between the Confederation and cantons is to be based as far as possible on the principle of subsidiarity.

Parliament did not accept that fiscal consolidation should involve significant tax increases. Virtually all the revenue measures proposed in the 1994 consolidation programme were rejected;[64] only the increase in tobacco tax and the reform of stamp duty were accepted, but the latter has no revenue implications. The expenditure measures requiring Parliament's approval (the first subsection in Table 16) were pared back from SF 740 million in 1997 to SF 540 million. This reflects a reduction in the targeted expenditure cuts from SF 490 million to SF 250 million (the social welfare measures and the termination of fuel tax refunds were rejected) partially offset by an increase (SF 50 million) in the linear cuts in subsidies to SF 300 million per year. The 1994 consolidation programme approved by Parliament reduces the primary deficit by SF 1.9 billion in 1998, SF 2 billion less than the reduction proposed by the Federal Council. Around one half of the estimated 1998 structural deficit before the 1994 consolidation programme (SF 4 billion) therefore remains.

The Confederation's medium-term financial plan[65]

As part of the budgetary process, the Federal Council prepares a medium-term financial plan based on the policies outlined in the budget including, in the case of the latest budget, the full implementation of the 1994 consolidation programme.[66] The current plan covers the period from 1996 to 1998 and is based on the assumptions that growth in real GDP averages 2 per cent per annum and that inflation averages 1.5 per cent. For the period 1994-1998, expenditures are projected to grow by 3.1 per cent per year, falling slightly as a proportion of GDP to 11.8 per cent, and revenues are projected to grow by 6.8 per cent per year, rising as a proportion of GDP to 11.3 per cent (Table 17). These trends imply a progressive reduction in the deficit from SF 6.5 billion (1.8 per cent of GDP) in 1995 (budget estimate) to SF 1.9 billion (0.5 per cent of GDP) in 1998. Gross debt in these projections peaks at 22.9 per cent of GDP in 1997; if, however, allowance were made for Parliament's rejection of much of the 1994 consolidation programme, the medium-term projections would show that debt still would not be stabilised as a percentage of GDP by 1998.

The only category of expenditure projected to decline in real terms is defence. With the exceptions of social welfare and transport, which are projected to stabilise, the other categories of expenditure are projected to grow in real terms. The most marked increase is for debt servicing, mainly reflecting the growing debt burden. The principal source of revenue for the Confederation, the turnover tax (ICHA) and its replacement, the VAT, are together projected to grow by 7.7 per cent per year over 1994-98, reflecting the increase in revenues

Table 17. **Growth in expenditures and revenues of the Confederation to 1998**

	1994-98 [1] Percentage change	1995	1998
		Budget structure	
Total expenditure	3.1	100.0	100.0
Social welfare	1.8	26.7	25.6
Transport	1.8	14.8	14.5
Defence	0.7	13.9	12.9
Research and education	3.9	7.5	7.7
Agriculture and food	2.7	8.0	7.7
Foreign affairs	3.1	5.1	5.0
Debt management and cantons' share			
of federal tax receipts	8.6	14.8	17.7
Other	2.8	9.2	8.8
Total receipts	6.8	100.0	100.0
Turnover tax/VAT	7.7	29.4	27.8
Federal income tax	5.8	23.7	24.5
Fuel taxes	9.3	12.3	12.4
Withholding tax	12.0	8.0	11.5
Stamp duty	4.1	5.1	4.3
Customs duty	7.4	3.3	3.4
Other taxes	1.9	6.5	15.0
Other receipts	4.9	11.7	11.0
		SF billion	
Total expenditure		42.9	48.2
Total receipts		36.4	46.3
Budget deficit		6.5	1.9
		Percentage of GDP	
Total expenditure		11.7	11.8
Total receipts		9.9	11.3
Budget deficit		1.8	0.5

1. Initial budget on initial budget.
Source: Swiss Confederation, *1995 Budget.*

(ranging from SF 1.6 billion in 1997 to SF 1.8 billion in 1998) resulting from the introduction of the VAT. High growth is also projected for the direct federal income tax, the Confederation's second biggest source of revenue, reflecting economic recovery, the effects from 1997 of moving to annual taxation for companies,[67] and the proposed introduction of proportional company income taxation. Withholding tax is projected to grow particularly strongly, mainly reflecting economic recovery (especially increasing dividends) and a decline in refunds as a percentage of receipts.[68]

The projected stability of social welfare expenditure, despite lower outlays for unemployment compensation, suggests that underlying pressures for increases in expenditures on social welfare remain intense. This category of expenditures grew by 50 per cent in real terms between 1980 and 1992, rising to 22.8 per cent of Confederation expenditure. Growth in this period was boosted by a number of discretionary decisions[69] but was not affected by loans to the unemployment insurance fund; these commenced in 1993. Abstracting from payments to the unemployment insurance fund, social welfare expenditure is projected to grow on average by 6.5 per cent per year from 1994 to 1998, with high growth projected for age pensions, invalidity pensions, and sickness benefits (Table 18). The exceptionally high growth rate (9.7 per cent per year) projected for payments for sickness insurance reflects the increased subsidies from 1996 which are a part of the revision of the sickness-insurance law which was accepted in a referendum in December 1994.

There is a risk that (what remains of) the financial plan may be optimistic about the growth in agricultural expenditure (2.7 per cent per year). Although substantial increases (8.0 per cent per year) in direct payments are projected, these are not sufficient to protect farmers' incomes in the face of the decline in prices consequent upon the implementation of the GATT agreement. Hence there is a risk that farmers may obtain more income support; however, this risk must be weighed against budgetary pressures and the possible unwillingness of the rest of

Table 18. **Social welfare expenditure**

	1995 Budget Percentage of total	1994-95[1] Percentage change
Total	100.0	1.8
Age insurance	37.7	5.7
Invalidity insurance	22.9	7.6
Sickness insurance	17.1	9.7
Unemployment insurance	3.7	−83.5
Aid to refugees in Switzerland	8.2	2.5

1. Initial budget on initial budget.
Source: Swiss Confederation, *1995 Budget.*

the population to pay for more assistance for farmers. On the other hand, the growth assumptions underlying the projections appear to be low, as they imply that there still would be a significant output gap in 1998.

Structural policies

Last year's OECD *Economic Survey of Switzerland* (Chapter III) discussed in some detail a variety of ongoing structural reform projects. Of these, the replacement of the old turnover tax on goods by a general value-added tax and the freedom of movement from one occupational pension fund to another without suffering financial loss ("portability of pensions") have come into effect on 1 January 1995. The latter reform should encourage occupational and geographical mobility. A law also came into force which allows the use of funds accumulated in the occupational old-age and survivors' pension scheme for the financing of owner occupied housing. The 10th revision of the compulsory old-age and survivors' insurance scheme (AVS) – under discussion for fifteen years now – was approved in a referendum on 25 June 1995. This reform provides for independent entitlements for couples, compensation for time spent out of the workforce to raise and educate children and a progressive increase in the retirement age for women to 64; the retirement age for men remains at 65.

The reform law on sickness insurance, which puts the financing of sickness insurance on a sounder footing, enhances competition between insurers and contains cost-control measures, was approved in a referendum on 4 December 1994 and is envisaged to come into force on 1 January 1996. However, the technical details of its implementation have not been resolved yet. The initial proposals submitted for comment in January 1995 to the political parties, the cantons and the concerned professions have been subject to severe criticism.

The government's new approach to agricultural reform, which is spelt out in the *Seventh Report on Agriculture,* seeks to de-emphasise the instrument of price support and instead to put more weight on direct income payments to farmers, while at the same time pursuing ecological objectives. A legislative package reflecting this orientation was rejected by the people and cantons in a referendum held on 12 March 1995. This package included a revised constitutional basis for agriculture as well as draft legislation aimed at more flexibility in the system of quantitative ceilings on milk production by allowing trade in milk production quotas; the third element of the package was the proposed introduction of a solidarity charge on farmers to finance the marketing of farm products by agricultural organisations. The government interprets the rejection of this package of reforms as an expression of the people's desire for a more market- and ecologically oriented agriculture, as indicated by an opinion poll taken after the referendum. Hence, the rejection of the legislative package is likely to strengthen and accelerate the reform process under way. The government is currently preparing the second step of this reform process aimed at laying the foundations for a sustainable and competitive agricultural sector.

The reform of the legislation on unemployment insurance was passed by Parliament in June 1995. The government's bill makes the receipt of insurance benefits after a certain period contingent upon participation in employment programmes or training measures. This is consistent with the notion that the structural part of unemployment has increased in recent years, so that microeconomic measures are needed to bring this part of unemployment down again. In addition, those leaving school and higher education will be eligible for unemployment benefits only after a period of up to one year (currently 20 days). This period ("délai d'attente") is to be determined by the Federal Council.

Because of the high deficit of the unemployment insurance system, the Federal Council adopted an emergency decree (*"arrêté urgent"*) which allowed the contribution rate to unemployment insurance to be raised from 2 to 3 per cent of the gross wage as from 1 January 1995. In addition, unemployment benefits will no longer be paid during the first week of unemployment, except for low-income earners. The emergency decree will be in force only until the end of 1995.

A major reform package – also discussed in previous *Surveys* – is the revitalisation programme which in general aims at the liberalisation of domestic markets. So far, only non-core elements of the programme have been implemented. Such reforms include the liberalisation of regulations concerning the employment of foreign specialists and of frontier workers, the removal of legal restrictions on sales and of technical barriers to parallel imports of private motor vehicles and the abolition of price regulations for car insurance. However, progress towards implementing core parts of the programme was made in June 1995, when the lower House of Parliament passed legislation strengthening the present competition law and removing obstacles to trade between cantons and when the upper House adopted a law on dismantling technical barriers to trade. Switzerland also became a member of the World Trade Organisation (WTO) the 1 July 1995, having made the necessary legislative changes. The government intends to build on the reforms in the agricultural sector and in public procurement associated with WTO membership; planned reforms would increase the market and environmental orientation of agriculture and would extend the field where law enforces public procurement on a competitive basis in the domestic market. A setback for the revitalisation programme was, however, the rejection in a public referendum on 25 June 1995 of proposals to ease the restrictions (Lex Friedrich) on foreign ownership of real estate.

The government is also engaged in bilateral negotiations with the European Union aimed at removing obstacles to market access on a mutual basis. These negotiations concern technical barriers to trade, public procurement, land and air transport, research, the free movement of people and market access for agricultural products.

A second set of reforms in the framework of the revitalisation programme was adopted by the Federal Council in June 1994. This new package focuses on various public-sector issues, many of them related to public-sector efficiency and new public management, which are dealt with in the next chapter.

III. Public sector efficiency and management

Introduction

The public sector produces a large and growing proportion of goods and services in most OECD countries, including Switzerland. These range from those non-market services provided in the general government sector, such as public administration and defence, to marketable services, such as telecommunications and postal services, and include merit goods, such as health and education. For the most part, the provision of these goods and services is not subject to the competitive disciplines found in other sectors. In these circumstances, there is a risk of inefficiencies involving excessive costs or inadequate tailoring of services to public needs. In addition to the production of government services, the public sector has a powerful influence on the economy through its management of regulation and competition policy. Previous surveys have concluded that policies in these areas have sheltered relatively large portions of the Swiss economy from competitive pressures.[70] In Switzerland, the sheltered sector includes many industries – railroads, telecommunications and electrical power generation – that are currently run as government-owned monopolies influenced (and sometimes protected) by various regulatory arrangements.

Concerns about public-sector management have been sharpened in recent years by several developments. First, political pressures for tighter fiscal control at all levels of government have emerged. Second, globalisation of business has obliged firms to seek improved performance from their suppliers, including those in the non-traded sector. Third, although Swiss voters have decided against membership of the European Economic Area, regulatory alignment with EU rules would facilitate ongoing trade and investment relationships and would ensure that the Swiss business sector is not unduly penalised by regulations that differ markedly in scope or content from those prevailing in other countries. Fourth, just as new technologies have allowed large parts of the private sector to restructure operations, it has become increasingly obvious that these same technologies can be used to streamline or to improve government operations. Fifth, structural change has undermined some sectors' status as "natural monopolies" and has created a need to realign the policy "mix" between regulation, competition and public ownership. Throughout the OECD area, such pressures have intensified the need for reform of the public sector to improve its efficiency and responsiveness to user demands. Switzerland has not been immune from these pressures and is increasingly making public sector reform a priority for economic policy.

This chapter is divided into two parts – the first deals with the general government sector and the second with public enterprises. The first part begins with a discussion of the organisation and scope of the general government sector, which comprises central and lower levels of government, including compulsory social security. Pressures for organisational changes are then discussed, followed by some of the ways in which the Swiss authorities have responded to these pressures. These responses have largely comprised reforms within traditional organisational structures but, in view of the limited scope to improve efficiency within such structures, are increasingly including reforms which overhaul government's organisational structure itself. The essence of such reforms, which are known as New Public Management (NPM), is that government agencies contract to supply certain outputs within a budget constraint and are free to decide how best to use the available resources to produce the contracted outputs. The second part of the chapter begins by outlining the nature of public enterprises in Switzerland and their organisational arrangements, followed by a discussion of the regulatory environment in which these businesses operate. The remainder of the chapter discusses regulatory and management arrangements for the main public enterprises and specific reforms which are under way or are being considered.

General government sector

Organisation and scope

As in other OECD countries, general government expenditure in Switzerland has expanded markedly in recent decades and now amounts to a substantial proportion of GDP. Current outlays (including compulsory social security) have doubled as a proportion of GDP since 1960, reaching 40 per cent in 1993 (Figure 18).[71] Around one-half of this increase is attributable to the rise in social security outlays. These grew strongly in the 1960s and 1970s, reflecting the maturing of the social security system[72] and its increasing generosity, including the introduction of unemployment insurance in the 1980s. Such outlays again increased markedly in the early 1990s, reaching 17 per cent of GDP in 1993,[73] owing mainly to the unprecedented levels of unemployment during this period but also to further enhancements in the system's benefits. Approximately one-half of the remaining increase in outlays is attributable to expenditures on personnel with the rest being spent on diverse current transfers. Growth in outlays has been most pronounced for the cantons and communes, which now account for 35 per cent and 29 per cent respectively of general government expenditures excluding social security. General government employment has also increased markedly, rising from 6.4 per cent of total employment in 1960 to an estimated 11.3 per cent in 1994[74] (Table 19) (although this remains well below the OECD average).

Figure 18. **TRENDS IN CURRENT OUTLAYS IN SWITZERLAND**
Per cent of GDP

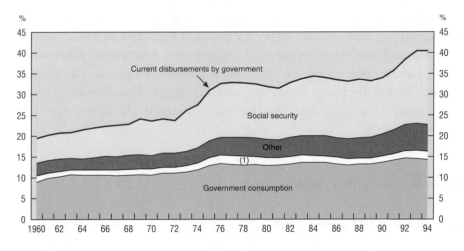

1. Property income paid by government.
Source: OECD.

Table 19. **Share of general government in total employment**

Per cent

	1960	1970	1980	1990	1991	1992	1993	1994
United States	12.7	16.0	16.4	15.5	15.7	15.9	15.8	15.5
Japan	..	7.7	8.8	8.1	8.1	8.1	8.2	8.4
Germany	8.1	11.2	14.6	15.1	15.9	16.1	16.1	16.2
France	..	17.9	20.3	22.6	22.8	23.3	24.1	24.4
Italy	9.1	12.3	15.7	17.1	17.0	17.2	17.9	18.1
United Kingdom	..	18.1	21.2	19.5	19.6	19.2	16.8	15.2
Canada	..	19.0	19.4	20.5	21.4	21.9	21.8	21.5
Australia	10.5	12.1	16.3	16.2	16.7	16.6	16.7	16.3
Austria	10.4	13.2	17.6	20.3	20.5	20.5	20.5	20.6
Belgium	11.7	13.6	18.7	19.5	19.1	19.1	19.2	18.8
Denmark	10.4	17.2	28.3	30.4	30.7	30.8	31.8	31.5
Finland	7.8	12.1	17.3	20.9	22.2	23.3	23.6	22.6
Greece	..	7.4	8.9	10.2	10.5	10.3	10.3	10.2
Iceland	..	12.4	15.7	18.4	18.5	18.5	18.7	18.5
Ireland	..	12.0	16.4	17.0	17.3	17.4	17.6	17.4
Luxembourg	..	..	..	..	..	..	..	..
Mexico	..	..	..	32.2	31.7	31.5	31.7	31.8
Netherlands	..	10.3	12.5	13.2	12.7	12.4	12.3	12.1
New Zealand	..	18.0	20.4	16.5	16.6	15.9	15.7	15.3
Norway	..	17.4	24.6	28.0	29.1	29.9	30.6	30.7
Portugal	4.9	7.9	10.7	14.7	14.8	18.3	18.1	18.1
Spain	..	4.9	9.0	13.4	13.9	14.3	14.8	14.8
Sweden	12.8	20.9	30.7	31.9	32.2	32.6	33.8	33.2
Switzerland [1]	**6.4**	**7.9**	**10.7**	**11.0**	**11.3**	**11.3**	**11.3**	**11.3**
Turkey	..	7.6	9.2	7.9	8.5	8.5	8.5	8.6

1.   Estimates based on census data.
Source: OECD.

As recently as 1990, Swiss current outlays as a percentage of GDP remained comfortably below the OECD average, but the growth of government expenditure in Switzerland in the past few years has been such that it has now reached a level broadly in line with the average of OECD countries (Table 20) – and thus, well below the average of EU countries but significantly above the United States and Japan. In terms of the composition of government expenditure, government consumption in Switzerland is about 3 percentage points of GDP less than the OECD average while social security and other current transfers are each about 2 percentage points higher; the latter category of transfers is surprisingly large in view of the Swiss government's low debt interest payments.

Table 20. **Current outlays, 1994**

Per cent of GDP

	Consumption	Social security	Other	Total
Switzerland	**14.2**	**17.7**	**8.5**	**40.4**
United States	17.4[1]	14.2	1.9	33.5[1]
Japan	9.8	12.8	5.5	28.2
Germany	19.3	17.7	8.8	45.8
France	20.0	23.3	7.7	51.0
Italy	17.3	19.5	14.0	50.8
United Kingdom	21.6	13.9	5.2	40.6
Canada	20.2	15.5	10.5	46.3
Australia	17.7	12.7	5.7	36.2
Austria	19.0	15.2	13.5	47.7
Belgium	15.3	22.4	17.2	54.9
Denmark	25.3	21.4	14.7	61.3
Finland	22.4	24.9	10.2	57.5
Greece	13.8	16.2	14.9	44.9
Iceland	19.9	6.2	7.0	33.0
Ireland	15.6	16.6	8.4	40.7
Netherlands	14.3	20.5	17.1	52.0
Norway	21.9	20.6	11.3	53.8
Portugal	16.7	12.0	14.8	43.6
Spain	17.0	16.7	9.0	42.7
Sweden	27.3	19.7	20.4	67.4
Total	16.8	15.8	6.5	39.1
EU (15)	19.2	18.7	10.3	48.3

1. Includes investment outlays.
Source: OECD.

Traditional management structures in the Swiss government sector, as in other OECD countries, were centralised (at each level of government), tended to be hierarchical, relied heavily on rules and emphasised processes rather than outcomes. Line managers had little scope to manage, with central management providing detailed prescriptions on how things were to be done, including what labour inputs were to be used and how they were to be remunerated. In this environment, line managers tended to not be held accountable for outcomes, only for whether they followed the rules. A corollary of the weak focus on the objectives of government expenditure was a lack of focus on the clients. Managers rarely asked themselves how clients' needs could be met more efficiently and had few channels for feedback from clients. It should be noted in this regard, however, that while there were few channels for clients individually to express their views about public services, the allocation of a large proportion of government expenditure in Switzerland to lower levels of government and the extensive use of referenda undoubtedly provided important channels unavailable in most other countries for clients to express their views collectively.

These management structures were developed in an era when management was considered to involve ensuring that the leadership's orders were put into effect. Leadership involved telling subordinates what to do rather than empowering them to achieve agreed objectives. Obedience rather than initiative was required from the managed. The army exemplified this approach to management, but it was also dominant in the private sector. The attraction for the government of this approach was that it seemed to be a low-cost way of ensuring that money was spent in a certain way, something which is not easy to ensure in an organisation as large and complex as government. Risks that government employees would misuse funds and, in particular, misappropriate them, were minimised. This "command and control" approach to management was mirrored in government regulation, which relied extensively on prescriptions rather than on incentives.

Just as traditional management structures in the private sector were found to be poorly adapted to meeting demands for increased efficiency, so too it has become increasingly evident that public sector structures are also unsuitable. These structures do not focus government employees on serving clients' needs, do not provide managers with the flexibility to decide how best to serve those needs and provide little scope to respond quickly to developments. In these circumstances outputs are unlikely to be well-adapted to clients' needs, which are changing continuously, and are unlikely to be produced at least cost. However, whereas private firms exposed to intensifying competition have been forced to restructure to enhance efficiency so as to survive, there is no corresponding direct pressure on the government sector. Restructuring in this sector only occurs when the pressure of public opinion forces governments to initiate fundamental reforms in government management practices.

Reforms within a traditional management structure

To date most reforms of the government sector in Switzerland have sought to achieve spending cut-backs within the confines of the government sector's traditional management structures. An early example of this approach was the Confederation's expenditure cuts in the 1970s, characterised as "cut-back management".[75] These were, however, largely ineffective because cuts in public investment were subsequently compensated for by increases or, in the case of cuts in transfers, by shifting the expenditure burden to lower levels of government or to households.[76] A similar approach was to place a ceiling on federal-employee numbers ("Personalstop") in 1974. This was subsequently (1983) developed into a rule that the number of federal employees could be increased only if it were not possible to release the required labour input from other tasks, whether by rationalisation of work organisation or by cutting out other tasks. Although there were initially some savings from this approach, they have not proved to be durable, as a variety of means have been employed to get around the ceilings; these include hiring personnel on a temporary basis and contracting out.

Another approach to slowing the growth in expenditure adopted by the federal government was to collect and analyse proposals made by staff on eliminating unnecessary tasks and carrying out others more efficiently. This approach, which was used in 1984 in the rationalisation programme for the federal administration (EFFI), turned out to be a partial success. No increase in staff numbers was required to compensate for a reduction in the working week from 44 to 42 hours and there was even some capacity to do additional tasks. However, the objectives of the programme, a 3 per cent reduction in staff numbers and a 5 per cent decline in working time, were not achieved.

The federal government returned to the issue of rationalising the administrative workload in 1989 with the launching of a study on this issue.[77] A number of rationalisation projects have emerged from this process and have already been implemented or are in the process of being implemented. These include the reorganisation of the Federal Military Department and a similar project for the Federal Department of Foreign Affairs. Economies from these projects, however, have been modest.

Following an initial series of pilot projects, the Federal Council decided in January 1991 to introduce "management controls" into federal administration. Management controls encompass accounting and information systems that allow ongoing activities to be evaluated, and associated incentive systems for ensuring that organisational objectives are being pursued. The Council has approved a number of projects that seek to evaluate the suitability of various methods of management control in particular government settings (examples include implementation of mountain subsidies, management of the Federal Railways and the Post and Telecommunications, management of development co-operation and humanitarian aid).

Towards New Public Management

While public sector efficiency undoubtedly could be improved within the existing institutional framework, governments in many OECD countries, including Switzerland, have concluded that significant improvements would require a change in the framework itself. The essence of this change is to move away from hierarchical organisations by more clearly defining the outputs expected from government organisations and by delegating decision-making responsibility about how best to deliver these outputs within a given budget constraint; concomitantly, public servants are required to be more accountable for outcomes. The emerging framework, which is known as New Public Management (NPM), aspires to create a fundamental change in the culture of the public sector. Instead of thinking in terms of due process and rigid frameworks for service provision, civil servants are encouraged to focus on improving outcomes for clients within budget constraints, including by exploring alternatives to direct public provision (see Box 3). Managers are required to manage.

Separating policy from administrative functions

A starting point for NPM reforms in a number of OECD countries has been the separation of policy from administrative functions.[78] This has the potential to strengthen both policy setting and administration, in particular by clarifying objectives and increasing flexibility in the means employed to achieve them. Policy makers can be more focused on selecting the objectives to be pursued, including ensuring that they are mutually consistent. The best means to realise these objectives can then be chosen from a range of alternatives rather than necessarily using the traditional supply channels. Administrators in turn are able to focus on how best to meet the output objectives set for them.

A reform of the federal administration which goes in this direction is under way. The principal objectives of this reform, for which the relevant law was submitted to Parliament in 1993 and should come into force in 1996, are to strengthen the policy making functions of the federal government and to adapt

Box 3. **Outsourcing**

There has been an increasing tendency in a number of OECD countries in recent years to contract out government services instead of producing them directly; this also has been a major feature of rationalisation in private firms. The potential advantage of this approach is that the production of services in the government sector is exposed to competitive pressure – unless public production is as efficient as private production, the job is moved to the private sector. In principle, the activities best suited to outsourcing are those for which the transactions costs of contracting with third parties are low. This tends to be the case for services with clearly definable outputs, such as rubbish collection. Standardised outputs in particular are easier to contract out than those which require unique specifications or organisational knowledge.

Outsourcing in the government sector in Switzerland is small relative to government production of services. In a recent survey[1] of communes with more than 5 000 inhabitants, it was found that around one-quarter of their services were provided through contracting out compared with almost two-thirds through public production (direct management or inter-commune co-operative production) (Table 21).[2] The services for which greatest resort to contracting out is made are waste collection, road maintenance, and school transport. Direct provision, on the other hand, is dominant for cleaning streets and public buildings, garden maintenance and computer services. The nature of the services still largely produced in the government sector suggests that considerable scope remains to expand outsourcing.[3]

There is only limited evidence in Switzerland on the comparative efficiency of public and private production. Two studies by Pommerehne (1976, 1983) showed that for waste collection the average cost of private production was about 10 per cent lower than for public provision.[4] In a more recent study, Burgat and Jeanrenaud (1990) found that private production was on average 40 per cent less expensive than public production. The main sources of the private sector's cost advantage were lower administration costs, lower wages and better exploitation of economies of scale.

A disturbing feature of outsourcing by the communes is that there is not greater use of competitive tendering. This gives rise to considerable variation in the economies actually realised through outsourcing. For example, Burgat and Jeanrenaud (1992) found huge differences in the efficiency of waste collection across municipalities, even though 57 out of the 98 municipalities included in the study contracted the service out. In another study, Jeanrenaud (1988) concluded that the absence of competitive tendering gave rise in some cases to substantial rents for private suppliers and, not surprisingly, was slowing innovation and improvements in productivity. This suggests that there is considerable scope to realise greater economies from outsourcing by adopting open, transparent processes for competitive tendering.

The effectiveness of outsourcing seems to have been limited by the authorities' failure to adapt contracts adequately to the nature of the service to be supplied privately. Moreover, in services supplied under conditions of natural monopoly (such as the distribution of energy, sewage disposal and the provision of regional infrastructure), the

(continued on next page)

(continued)

transaction costs associated with designing contracts which adequately ensure that private firms' interests overlap with public interests has encouraged many municipalities to opt for direct provision. In such cases, efficiency gains can be obtained more easily by establishing co-operative arrangements with neighbouring municipalities or by territorial merger of facilities.

---

1. Schwab, N. and L. Christie (1990).
2. The other major mechanisms were inter-commune co-operation and the granting of concessions.
3. Outsourcing could easily be expanded for rubbish collection, transport services and the management of sport and leisure facilities.
4. Pommerehne, W. (1976). In a subsequent study, the author observed that the average cost of waste collection in municipalities which make decisions in assemblies of citizens (direct democracy) is 29 per cent lower than in municipalities with an elected Parliament (representative democracy). See W. Pommerehne (1983).

better its administrative structures to the requirements of future government activity. It is proposed to alleviate the administrative work load of the policy branch of government by creating secretaries of state and improving organisation. With respect to administrative activities, the aim is to eliminate the doubling up of tasks, improve co-ordination and coherence, take advantage of synergies and clearly attribute tasks and responsibilities.

A mandate for outputs within a budget constraint

The Confederation has taken NPM reforms further in a pilot project concerning the office of intellectual property rights (Office fédéral de la propriété intellectuelle (OFPI)). This office was transformed into an institute (Institut de la propriété intellectuelle (IPI)), given its own legal identity and a mandate for the services to be provided. Compared to the OFPI, the IPI has more discretion to decide how to achieve its objectives.

The Federal Council recently announced its intention to give certain other offices mandates to deliver specified outputs within multi-year budgets.[79] The offices concerned then will be free to decide how best to use their budgets to deliver the agreed outputs. An immediate advantage of the proposed reform is that wasteful expenditures at the end of the year to ensure that the budget is

Table 21. **Method of service provision**

Per cent

Services	Direct management	Intercommunal co-operation	Contracting out	Concession	Subsidies	Coupons	Volunteers	Market
Garbage collection	29.7	20.3	43.9	5.4	0.0	0.0	0.0	0.4
Snow removal	66.2	1.0	30.4	1.7	0.0	0.0	0.0	0.7
Urban heating	52.5	10.0	15.0	10.0	2.5	0.0	0.0	10.0
Road maintenance	64.6	0.0	33.0	0.0	0.3	0.0	0.0	2.1
Road cleaning	87.6	0.0	11.1	0.5	0.0	0.0	0.0	0.9
Park and garden maintenance	74.1	0.0	23.9	0.4	0.4	0.0	0.4	0.8
Ambulance services	22.5	30.5	29.1	4.0	5.3	0.0	4.6	4.0
Removal of carcasses	33.6	43.8	17.1	0.5	2.3	0.0	0.5	2.3
School transport	37.1	3.3	33.8	11.3	5.3	4.0	3.3	2.0
Public transport	7.4	21.2	21.2	28.6	18.5	1.1	0.0	2.1
Kindergarten	80.2	2.4	1.4	0.0	11.8	0.0	2.8	1.4
Cable network	24.9	9.2	9.2	46.5	0.0	0.0	1.1	9.2
Computer services	68.4	10.5	16.4	1.2	0.0	0.0	0.0	3.5
Cleaning of public buildings	76.6	0.4	20.1	0.0	0.0	0.0	0.0	2.9
Laundry	35.6	30.1	27.4	0.0	0.0	0.0	0.0	6.8
Restaurant service	47.1	28.6	12.9	0.0	2.9	0.0	5.7	2.9
Cantines	35.7	0.0	17.9	7.1	10.7	0.0	7.1	21.4
Water distribution	65.2	13.4	12.1	6.7	0.9	0.0	0.9	0.9
Electricity distribution	40.3	2.4	22.7	33.2	0.0	0.0	0.0	1.4
Gas distribution	34.2	5.1	29.7	29.1	0.0	0.0	0.0	1.9
Average	52.5	10.2	22.3	8.9	2.5	0.2	0.8	2.5

Source: Schwab and Christie (1990).

Box 4. **Public enterprises of the canton of Bern**

The canton of Bern is currently reviewing its participation in public and private enterprises and to this end commissioned a report from an *ad hoc* group of experts. The report includes an exhaustive list of share holdings as at December 1994. This shows that Bern has investments in around 140 enterprises. These investments can be classified as follows:

- *i)* Public establishments and majority interests:
  - the cantonal bank;
  - the power generation company;
  - and 5 other enterprises.
- *ii)* Public establishment with a legal monopoly:
  - the fire insurance company.
- *iii)* Majority interests (Confederation, canton and communes):
  - 27 regional public transport companies.
- *iv)* Minority interests:
  - 46 enterprises including the Swiss National Bank, air transport companies (Swissair and Crossair), home-owner co-operatives and sugar production companies;
  - real-estate interests: 5 enterprises;
  - compulsory interests: 55 enterprises, mostly agricultural co-operatives.

These investments are valued at around SF 825 million, including a SF 607 million stake in the cantonal bank. In most cases, the canton is represented by one or more members on the Board.[1]

The report of the group of experts contains the following main criticisms of these investments:

- a certain number of them are not necessary in the public interest and many others lack clear objectives;
- there is no permanent inventory of the canton's investments and its representatives on the boards of directors;
- several enterprises and/or their Board members are financially interrelated;
- the separation between political and business responsibilities is not clearly drawn;
- the Boards tend to be too large to carry out their functions efficiently;
- the representatives of the canton in the Boards are often appointed for political reasons and not for their competence.

The group of experts made the following recommendations concerning cantonal policy in respect of its investments in enterprises:

- the canton should acquire a business interest or run a public enterprise only if there is a clear public objective to be met which cannot be achieved efficiently in any other way;

(continued on next page)

(continued)

    –   the usefulness of the interests and public enterprises should be re-examined every year;

    –   the canton should review its different interests in firms belonging to the same function (*e.g.* transport) in view of a potential merger or collaboration;

    –   the Board members should be appointed for their business competence;

    –   all important decisions on interests and public enterprises should be taken by the government at the highest level;

    –   all interests (except those held for portfolio investment) should be listed in the annual report of the government, including the accounts of the major companies.

This review of the Canton's share holdings will be completed by the summer of 1995. An early opportunity to put the recommendations of the experts' report into effect will be in 1996, when new Board members are scheduled to be appointed.[2] The gradual reduction of the Canton's share holdings, however, could take a few years to accomplish.

---

1.   There are estimated to be over 100 persons representing the canton on different boards.

2.   The decision has been taken to reduce the number of Board members to 9 by the year 2000.

exhausted will be avoided. The offices affected by this proposal will be required to present financial accounts to Parliament.

Similar initiatives are also being introduced at the municipal and cantonal levels: the cantons of Bern (canton, city of Bern and some municipalities), Lucerne, St. Gallen, Valais and Zurich (health sector) are experimenting with such reforms. The canton of Valais has gone farthest with these reforms, having re-examined its whole administration and commenced planning to implement measures which will reduce public employment by around 10 per cent. The canton of Bern also is currently preparing a reform package to put NPM reforms into effect in its administration. This will result in a change in the distribution of tasks between the canton and the municipalities, the partial privatisation of its cantonal bank and a systematic evaluation of its participation in private-sector activities (Box 4). The city of Bern launched its concept of NPM[80] at the beginning of 1995, with the start of three pilot projects in the following areas: fire-brigade, rubbish collection and youth protection. The results will be assembled and presented in a report by the end of 1996. A feature of these pilot projects is an inquiry into user satisfaction with the relevant services, the results of which will be published this year. As of January 1996, the canton of Lucerne also will commence nine pilot projects in NPM covering a wide spectrum of services: schools, museums, the statistical office, automobile inspection (service des automobiles), property management and environmental protection. Progress on these experiences will be reported regularly in annual government statements, with a final evaluation scheduled for 1999.

Public enterprises

Public enterprises produce goods and services which are sold in markets. Government ownership of these businesses ranges from a significant minority holding, such as Swissair, to outright ownership, as in the case of the PTT (postal and telecommunications services) and the CFF (railways). Public enterprises may be organised as corporations and subject to the law for private corporations or to public law. Alternatively, they may be organised as public establishments, as are the PTT and CFF, and subject to public law rather than company law.

As in many other OECD countries, public enterprises dominate the industries which supply infrastructure services (Figure 19). The postal services, railways, telecommunications, and electricity industries are more than three quarters owned by government in Switzerland. Compared with other OECD countries, public ownership in infrastructure industries in Switzerland is high; this is especially so for electricity and telecommunications. In addition to the four industries referred to above, the government has a significant stake in banking through the cantonal banks and the deposit-taking services of the PTT and in insurance, through the cantonal fire insurance companies, which are monopoly suppliers of fire insurance in most cantons.

As infrastructure services, especially telecommunications services, are an increasingly important business input, the search by companies facing international competition for improved performance from their suppliers has inevitably led to calls for better infrastructure services at lower prices. Moreover, budgetary pressures have made governments less willing to accept sub-standard returns on

81

Figure 19. **OWNERSHIP OF INDUSTRIES IN SELECTED OECD COUNTRIES**
May 1992

	Postal services	Railways	Telecom-munications	Electricity	Gas production	Airlines
SWITZERLAND						
Australia						
Canada						
United States						
New Zealand						
United Kingdom						
Japan						
Austria						
France						
Norway						
Italy						
Denmark						
Western Germany						
Netherlands						
Sweden						
Spain						
Belgium						

Note: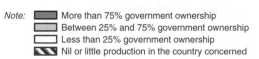
More than 75% government ownership
Between 25% and 75% government ownership
Less than 25% government ownership
Nil or little production in the country concerned

Source: EPAC, *Profitability and Productivity of Government Business Enterprises,* Research Paper No. 2, 1992.

their investments in these industries. The Swiss authorities are responding to these pressures by increasing competition in parts of these industries and by restructuring the businesses. In the case of Switzerland, another pressure is the desire to bring its regulatory framework for these industries into conformity with that in the EU. This is forcing the pace of change in some industries,[81] such as the telecommunications, as EU law is being reformed to facilitate greater competition in infrastructure industries. After briefly examining the regulatory environment in which most public enterprises operate, developments in the major public enterprises or industries dominated by government ownership are reviewed in the remainder of this chapter.

Government ownership as a regulatory device

Most of the industries in which government has a substantial stake in Switzerland have traditionally been viewed as natural monopolies; the principal exceptions are the cantonal banks, the cantonal fire insurance companies and the banking activities of the PTT. Government ownership has been adopted effectively in most cases as a means of regulating such industries. Resort to government ownership presumably reflected a view that this form of control was likely to be less costly than regulating privately-owned monopolies.

Ownership as a substitute for regulation of natural monopolies has been an important feature in most OECD countries, as demonstrated by the high levels of public ownership in such industries (see Figure 19). But this view has been changing. The assumption that a publicly owned firm necessarily acts in the public interest is now widely considered to be implausible.[82] A consideration of the incentives facing the management and workers in a public enterprise suggests that it is more likely that they will seek to appropriate the monopoly rents through better pay and working conditions than would otherwise be possible.[83] From this point of view, regulation is vital for both publicly- and privately-owned natural monopolies to ensure that they do not exploit their market power.

There has also been a realisation that only parts of these industries have natural monopoly characteristics. In particular, transmission networks are often natural monopolies but the other services produced in the industry concerned are potentially competitive. For example, electricity distribution is a natural monopoly but generation can be competitive. Many OECD countries, including Switzerland, are now considering how to separate such elements of these industries and introduce regulations which ensure fair access to common facilities, such as transmission networks, while creating contestable markets for the other services. This trend has in many cases also been accompanied by privatisation.

Regulatory framework

Public enterprises in Switzerland are, in so far as they are not exposed to adequate competition, subject to price surveillance. The price surveillance authority[84] has the power to recommend against price increases which it considers to be an abuse of monopoly power but cannot prevent the increases from coming into effect. In making its recommendation, the price surveillance authority must take into account not only the considerations relevant to the economic state of the enterprise or the national economy, but also requirements flowing from other government policies; these include agricultural policy, transport policy, energy policy, public health, environmental protection, and social or cultural policy. The price surveillance authority may only publish recommendations for which an amicable agreement has been reached with the party investigated.

Monopolies are clearly subject to less control from a central regulator in Switzerland than in most other OECD countries. The price surveillance authority has no power to block price increases which it considers to be abusive, all manner of poorly defined policy interests can be invoked to justify a price increase and only those recommendations amicably settled can be published. Such regulation is unlikely to be effective against the abuse of monopoly power and is certainly not transparent.

There are no laws in Switzerland to ensure access to common facilities, such as transmission networks, on a fair and efficient basis. This is likely to change, however, at least in the telecommunications industry (see below), so as to conform with the envisaged reform of EU laws in this domain.

Postal and telecommunication services

Profitability

Postal and telecommunications services are largely supplied under monopoly conditions by the PTT, a government business enterprise (*régie fédérale*). It made small profits in 1993 and 1994 (Table 22) after three successive annual losses. A decomposition of the operating results for the two main departments ("centres de profits"), namely telecommunications ("Télécom PTT") and postal services ("La Poste"), shows that the former is quite profitable and the latter is unprofitable.[85] Profitability for Télécom PTT is supported by a growing international market for telecommunication services and a low cost of capital in a capital-intensive industry; the PTT raises most of its finance from low-yielding postal deposit accounts.[86] In contrast, postal services are labour-intensive and operate in a stagnant market. Moreover, they are obliged to operate two loss-making services of public interest ("prestations en faveur de l'économie génér-

Table 22. **Financial accounts of the Swiss PTT, 1994**

SF millions

	PTT[1]		La Poste	Télécom PTT
	1993	1994	1994	1994
Turnover growth (per cent)	1.0	2.0	0.0	3.0
Total sales	13 593	13 926	5 467	9 748
Total expenses	13 403	13 623	5 589	8 693
Profit	190	303	–122	1 055
Profit to turnover (per cent)	1	2	–2	11
Cash flow	3 230	3 591	242	3 812
Investment	2 943	2 864	4 402	2 376
Coverage rate (per cent)	110	125	55	160
Balance sheet total	24 994	28 049	24 158	15 733
Own capital	1 805	1 805	290	1 446
Employees	62 215	60 208	39 039	20 092

1. Including the directorship.
Source: PTT Annual Report, 1994.

ale'') – the postal bus network, which offers services which are complementary to the national railway system; and newspaper delivery by mail at prices below cost.

Organisational arrangements

The federal government and Parliament play a significant role in the management decisions of the PTT. The resulting constraints on the PTT management's decision-making powers include the following:

- the federal Parliament and government both have an influence on marketing policy;
- prices are fixed by the Government, usually with a lag of more than a year between the proposal and the implementation;
- both the level and the structure of prices have to be uniform across the country; under these circumstances, price-differentiation (*e.g.* according to customer size) is difficult to achieve;
- the budget, the annual accounts and the destination of profits must be approved by the Parliament;
- the firm has no access to national or international capital markets;
- wages are fixed by the Federal Council;

- directors are appointed by the federal government, even at the district level;
- the firm cannot by itself own other companies or establish joint ventures; agreements and contracts with foreign partners must be concluded by the federal government.

These arrangements clearly are not conducive to efficiency or flexibility. Nor are they consistent with the requirements for greater competition in the market for telecommunications, a challenge which must be met if Switzerland is to reform this market in line with the planned liberalisation in EU countries. The Swiss authorities recognise the need for reform in the telecommunications market and have commenced reforms of the PTT to facilitate the move towards the regulatory framework envisaged in the EU reform.[87] A first step in this regard was the implementation of the organisational reform project for the PTT known as "optimisation des structures de gestion" between January 1993 and the end of 1994. The main objective of the project was to improve client services. This was to be done principally by decentralising responsibilities and simplifying cumbersome administrative procedures.[88] The postal and telecommunication services of the PTT were separated into two distinct entities – *La Poste* and *Télécom PTT* – and the newly-created departments were given more decision-making autonomy. Specific management tools also were introduced in order to improve the monitoring of operations.

The second and more far-reaching stage of the reorganisation of the PTT (Project "TOP") is to give it the characteristics of a private company in so far as that is possible within the confines of the Federal Constitution.[89] Reforms being discussed in this context include: defining the basic services to be provided throughout the country; giving management the authority to set prices (in conformity with the principles of the Federal Constitution) and to decide on co-operation with other firms; giving management greater autonomy in financial and personnel affairs, including remuneration policies. This will require a total revision of the law on the organisation of PTT. The new law is expected to come into effect in 1998. Total privatisation of *Télécom PTT* is envisaged eventually.

La Poste – the cost of non-commercial services

A substantial proportion of the losses made by *La Poste* is attributable to the cost of non-commercial services it is obliged to provide. The most important of these are the delivery of the 1.2 billion newspapers per year at subsidised rates and the maintenance of unprofitable bus services. Subsidised newspaper delivery, which is supported in order to maintain a diversified press,[90] cost SF 269 million in 1993, a cost which is entirely borne by the PTT. This operational loss is to be reduced from 1996 onwards and the cost to be covered equally by the publishers, *La Poste* and the Confederation. With respect to postal bus services, which are largely contracted out,[91] the loss has been increasing in recent years, reaching some SF 180 million in 1993. This service is intended to support the objectives of Swiss regional policy by providing a reliable and relatively cheap means of transport, especially for villages and towns in mountain areas. In future, the cost of bus services provided in the public interest will be paid by the state.

Télécom PTT – liberalisation, service quality and pricing

In view of the importance of efficient telecommunications services to a modern economy[92] and of the rapid changes the sector in undergoing, the search for appropriate policies in this sector has become a matter of some urgency. The telecommunications market was partially liberalised in May 1992 when the new law on telecommunications ("Loi sur les télécommunications") came into effect. This totally liberalised the market for end-user equipment, subject only to the certification of devices by the Federal Office of Communication. Monopoly restrictions on service provision were also eliminated with the exception of voice telephony and infrastructure, where market access continues to be prohibited.[93] *Télécom PTT* retains its monopoly on the cable and hertzian infrastructure as well as on mobile communications. Overall, the telecommunications market is less competitive in Switzerland than in many other OECD countries (Table 23). Considerable scope remains for liberalisation in Switzerland.

The quality and universality of telephone services, while good, are not in all respects up to the standards which might be expected in view of Switzerland's high per capita income. The number of mainlines per 100 people – at 58 in 1990 – is among the highest in the OECD area. However, the household penetration rate is – at 89.8 per cent – the same as the OECD average. Switzerland's penetration ratio is below those of many other OECD countries with significantly lower per capita incomes (Table 24). Other quality indicators also place the Swiss telecommunications at about the average in OECD rankings. Figure 20 shows that the Swiss reported 40 faults per 100 main lines in 1992

Table 23.   **Status of facilities competition in the OECD area, 1994**

	PSTN[1] competition			Data comm. and leased lines		Mobile communication			Equipment
	Local	Trunk	Intl.	X.25[2]	LLs	Anal.	Digl.	Paging	CPE[3]
Switzerland	M	M	M	M	M	M	M	C	C
Australia	D	D	D	D	D	D	C	C	C
Austria	M	M	M	M	M	M	M	C	C
Belgium	M	M	M	1993	M	M	M	M	C
Canada	M	C	M[4]	C	C	RD	D	C	C
Denmark	M	M	M	1993	M	D	C	M	C
Finland	C	C	C	C	C	D	D	D	C
France	M	M	M	1993	M	D	D	D	C
Germany	M	M	M	C	M	M	D	1994	C
Greece	M	M	M	1997	M	–	D	M	C
Iceland	M	M	M	M	M	M	M	M	C
Ireland	M	M	M	1993	M	M	M	M	C
Italy	M	M	M	1993	M	M	D (1994)	M	C
Japan	C	C	C	C	C	RD	C	C	C
Luxembourg	M	M	M	1993	M	M	M	M	C
Netherlands	M	M	M	1993	M	M	D (1994)	1993	C
New Zealand	C	C	C	C	C	C	C	C	C
Norway	M	M	M	1993	M	M	D	1993	C
Portugal	M[5]	M	M[5]	C	M[5]	M	D	C	C
Spain	M	M	M	C	M	M	M	C	C
Sweden	C	C	C	C	C	C	C	C	C
Turkey	M	M	M	M	M	M	M	M	C
United Kingdom	C	C	D	C	C	D	C	C	C
United States	PC	C	C	C	C	RD	C	C	C

Key: C = Competition; D = Duopoly; PC = Partial competition; RD = Regional duopoly; M = Monopoly; 199x = Competition
    expected to be introduced this year.
1. Public switch telecommunications network.
2. X.25 is a standard for data transfer.
3. Customer premises equipment.
4. Intercontinental. Canada-US traffic, which constitutes 70 per cent of Canada originated international traffic is handled by
    Stentor regional telcos, Unitel and resellers on a competitive basis. Intercontinental (non-Canada-US) facilities based traffic
    is carried by Teleglobe; international resale has been allowed in Canada since 1991.
5. Exclusive rights of PTOs according to their respective concessions. For local and regional service Telecom Portugal and
    Telefones de Lisboa. For international Telecom Portugal and Comphania Portuguesa Radio Macroni.
Source: OECD.

(which is well above the OECD average), while 86.8 per cent of faults were corrected by the next working day (which is about average). As regards the number of leased lines – which in countries like Switzerland where private companies' right to build private networks is restricted indicates the extent to which private businesses can tailor networks to their own specific needs – Switzerland ranks fifth out of fifteen countries (Table 25).

Table 24. **Mainline penetration and universal service provision**

	Mainlines per 100 people		Household penetration[1]
	1989	1990	1989/90
Switzerland	**56.3**	**58.0**	**89.8**
Australia	45.2	47.1	93.3 (1989)
Austria	40.7	41.8	n.a.
Belgium	37.7	39.3	n.a.
Canada	53.0	57.5	108.5
Denmark	55.5	56.6	103.6
Finland	52.0	53.5	94.4
France	48.0	49.8	97.7 (1988)
Germany[2]	46.5	47.4	90.7 (1988)
Greece	37.7	38.9	89.0
Iceland	48.0	51.4	114.2
Ireland	25.7	28.1	67.6
Italy	37.0	38.8	86.7
Japan	42.3	43.5	87.1 (1989)
Luxembourg	46.8	48.2	95.4
Netherlands	45.1	46.4	86.1
New Zealand	42.5	43.6	97.2
Norway	49.0	50.3	92.4
Portugal	21.0	24.1	54.5 (1989)
Spain	30.3	32.3	79.0 (1989)
Sweden	67.3	68.3	121.0
Turkey	10.6	12.4	40.8
United Kingdom	43.5	44.2	86.4 (1988)
United States	45.4	45.3	93.3
OECD	41.5	42.6	89.1

1. (Number of mainlines used by residential users)/(number of households). OECD average includes 1989 data for Australia, Japan, Portugal and Spain, and 1988 data for France, Germany and the United Kingdom.
2. Before reunification.
Source: OECD, ITU, NTIA, FCC.

In preparation for increased competition, cross-subsidisation of services has been reduced. This has involved, in particular, price rebalancing with increases in prices for domestic calls and reductions for international calls. Measured at PPP exchange rates, Swiss telecommunications prices are now close to the OECD average for domestic calls but below average for international calls (Table 26).[94] While prices may still be about average, the trend in these prices since 1990 – compared with other countries – is definitely moving against Switzerland. This is particularly pronounced for business services, where an index of total charges for business telecommunications increased by 19 per cent in Switzerland over the

Figure 20. **QUALITY OF SERVICE IN SELECTED MEMBER COUNTRIES**

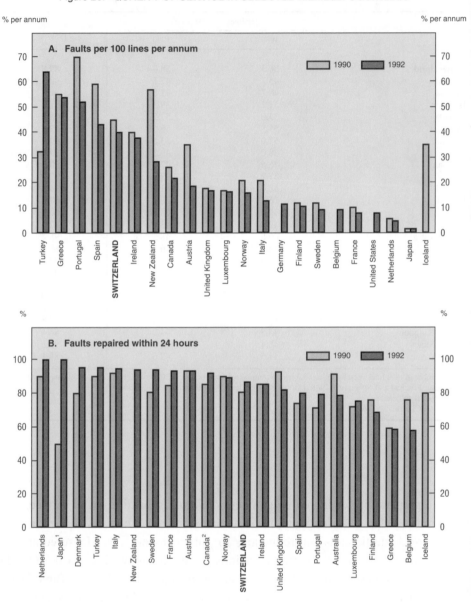

1. Approximation for 1992.
2. For business in 1992; the fault repair rate for households is 85.1 per cent in 1992.
Source: OECD, *Communication Outlook, 1995,* Table 6.4. See this table for more information about these data.

Table 25. **Leased line connections as a percentage of telecommunications mainlines**

	1992
Switzerland	**2.08**
United Kingdom [1]	2.96
Finland [1]	2.82
Belgium	2.47
Ireland	2.39
Germany [2]	2.00
Norway	1.86
Sweden [1]	1.47
Italy	1.24
Netherlands	1.05
Denmark	0.98
Austria	0.94
France	0.87
Portugal [3]	0.67
Spain	0.65

1. Had leased line facilities competition in 1992.
2. Estimate.
3. 1991 mainlines.
Source: OECD.

Table 26. **Charges for telecommunications services in Switzerland** [1]

Per cent of OECD average

	January 1994	
	Actual exchange rates [2]	Exchange rates [2] based on PPPs
All calls		
Business	115.3	96.1
Residential	121.8	101.5
International calls		
Business	101.1	84.2
Residential	97.0	81.0

1. Charges for baskets for calls. For a full description of the tariff comparison methodology for these and other baskets, please see OECD, ICCP Series No. 22, "Performance Indicators for Public Telecommunications operators".
2. 1993 exchange rates.
Source: OECD, *Communications Outlook 1995.*

Table 27. **Series index of business "telecommunications basket" total charges** [1]

	1990	1991	1992	1993	1994
Switzerland	**100.0**	**103.13**	**115.64**	**116.86**	**119.41**
Australia (Telstra)	100.0	109.28	112.29	111.85	108.49
Austria	100.0	100.05	91.39	88.20	86.84
Belgium	100.0	98.72	98.98	98.99	100.98
Canada (Bell Canada)	100.0	95.56	93.95	96.17	98.41
Denmark	100.0	108.18	107.04	108.09	107.27
Finland (HTC)	100.0	115.15	106.04	105.23	87.83
France	100.0	101.54	102.46	102.30	96.59
Germany	100.0	85.96	84.44	82.86	82.47
Greece	100.0	106.47	97.35	92.31	113.18
Iceland	100.0	71.93	85.71	91.11	92.30
Ireland	100.0	104.09	84.95	86.74	83.03
Italy	100.0	108.64	106.09	103.41	102.51
Japan (NTT)	100.0	91.25	91.73	93.17	80.44
Luxembourg	n.a.	n.a.	n.a.	n.a.	n.a.
Netherlands	100.0	100.24	104.23	101.85	109.56
New Zealand (TCNZ)	100.0	113.05	98.24	90.86	88.91
Norway	100.0	68.26	64.45	65.77	53.89
Portugal (TP/TLP)	100.0	102.85	93.29	91.25	92.55
Spain	100.0	116.45	113.33	115.36	114.54
Sweden (Telia)	100.0	114.79	102.68	101.10	86.71
Turkey	100.0	133.11	122.83	109.72	107.14
United Kingdom (BT)	100.0	98.63	99.03	95.73	88.33
United States (Nynex)	100.0	100.00	101.00	95.24	88.68
OECD average	100.0	102.06	99.01	97.57	95.22
Weighted average	100.0	99.78	99.26	96.60	91.45

1. Data is from business tariff basket. The basket is expressed in the form of an index that makes 1990 = 100. The weighted average is calculated with 1992 telecommunication mainlines.
Source: OECD.

four years to 1994, compared with a 9 per cent decline in the OECD average (Table 27). This relative deterioration is a general feature of non-competitive systems: they have not been as successful as competitive systems in translating technological progress into lower prices for customers (Figure 21). For a country whose most important business sectors rely heavily on telecommunication services, this is a serious emerging impediment to better economic performance.

Railways

The railways system in Switzerland is comprised of the federal railways – the CFF (Chemins de fer fédéraux) – which is a public enterprise entirely

Figure 21. **TOTAL COMMUNICATIONS CHARGES:
COMPETITIVE VERSUS NON-COMPETITIVE SYSTEMS**

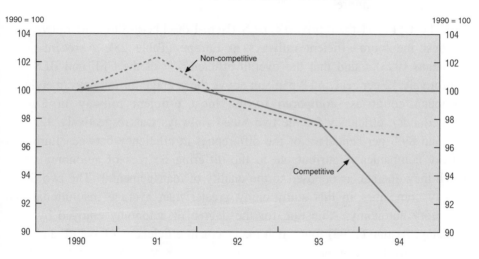

Source: OECD, *Communication Outlook, 1995,* Table 5.13. See this table for more information about these data.

owned by the Confederation, and a number of smaller regional semi-private[95] companies.[96] As in other countries, the decline in the demand for railway services relative to other modes of transport, especially road transport, has weighed on the CFF's profitability; it runs at a loss (SF 98 million in 1993). Most regional railways also run at a loss with this generally being covered, for the most part, by the Confederation and the cantons.

The Confederation compensates rail companies for operating unprofitable non-commercial services (''prestations en faveur de l'économie générale''); these include some regular services and non profitable lines maintained for regional policy purposes.[97, 98] It also makes substantial contributions towards infrastructure investment; these contributions amounted to SF 1.3 billion in 1993. This is set to escalate as the Alpine rail project[99] gets under way, although the details of its financing are being re-examined. Substantial investment also will be required for the realisation of the ''Railways 2000'' project, which is aimed at improving services on existing tracks, although it is hoped to finance this invest-

93

ment from improved operating results at the CFF and from reductions in other investment expenditures.

The CFF and the "private" BLS (Bern-Lötschberg-Simplon) railway are amongst the more efficient railways in Europe (Table 28). A recent study (Pestieau, 1993) found that the overall efficiency[100] of the CFF and BLS was respectively 12 per cent and 8 per cent above the average for railways in eighteen European countries; compared to the most efficient railway in Europe (Netherlands), efficiency for the two Swiss railways was respectively 92.5 per cent and 89.8 per cent. Part of the differences in efficiency between European railway companies is attributable to the differing degrees of autonomy under which they operate, as opposed to the quality of management.[101] The two Swiss railway companies in this study enjoy greater than average institutional and regulatory autonomy. Adjusting for the degree of autonomy enjoyed by each company, Pestiau (1993) found that management efficiency at the CFF and BLS was respectively 9 per cent above the average and 8 per cent below the average for the companies included in the study (Table 29); compared to the most efficiently managed railway company in Europe (Turkey), management efficiency was respectively 92.9 per cent and 78.8 per cent.

A recent study concluded that the efficiency of the regional railways[102] could be enhanced by involving cantons and regions in the determination and financing of services (following the benefit principle) and by defining clearly non-commercial service obligations, which should be paid for by government (Confederation and cantons). These two measures were also proposed in June 1993 by an internal "Groupe de réflexion" on the future of the CFF. The other major proposals made in respect of the CFF were:

- to increase taxation of heavy vehicles and private transportation in order to help cover infrastructure costs;
- to introduce a service contract between the Confederation and the CFF, which would clearly stipulate the objectives to be pursued and confer more freedom on management (to make decisions on issues such as the introduction of new products, contracting out, concentrating on services in which the CFF has a comparative advantage);
- to separate operating and infrastructure accounts and change accounting and financial management in order to be able to respond rapidly to changes in the market place.

Table 28. Efficiency measures of European railways, 1962-88

| Railway | | Average output (t-km) | | Efficiency[2] 1986-88 | Parametric frontier (DOLS)[1] | | |
		Passenger	Freight		Efficiency change	Technical progress	Total factor productivity change
		Millions			1962-88		
BLS	**Switzerland**	**4.9**	**1.1**	**0.71512**	**0.35837**	**0.43598**	**0.79435**
BR	United Kingdom	343.6	104.2	0.74568	0.52597	0.65920	1.18517
CFF	**Switzerland**	**64.1**	**28.0**	**0.73723**	**-0.07962**	**0.62466**	**0.54504**
CFL	Luxembourg	2.9	1.5	0.56206	-0.34547	0.65486	0.30936
CH	Greece	12.8	3.2	0.56406	-0.16666	1.71960	1.55294
CIE	Ireland	7.6	4.3	0.73113	0.37976	1.50182	1.88158
CP	Portugal	24.5	6.2	0.69245	0.30063	0.77754	1.07817
DB	Germany	384.7	196.3	0.61986	-0.08268	0.68657	0.60389
DSB	Denmark	35.7	8.3	0.52334	-0.34987	0.74256	0.39269
FS	Italy	210.3	60.3	0.63757	-0.03596	0.66529	0.62934
NS	Netherlands	82.6	15.3	0.79671	-0.06832	0.40904	0.34071
NSB	Norway	22.9	10.2	0.51639	0.01751	0.40051	0.41802
OBB	Austria	56.4	33.6	0.59374	-0.13622	0.69698	0.56075
RENFE	Spain	85.0	44.3	0.64701	0.81055	0.54393	1.35448
SJ	Sweden	64.1	40.7	0.66166	0.23506	0.28648	0.52154
SNCB	Belgium	64.4	21.9	0.62958	-0.15624	0.61799	0.45875
SNCF	France	261.3	204.1	0.73086	-0.06412	0.58146	0.51134
TCDD	Turkey	20.7	18.2	0.76936	-0.00743	1.30054	1.29311
VR	Finland	25.2	18.4	0.65256	-0.22642	0.84706	0.62064

1. Displaced ordinary least squares.
2. Efficiency relates outputs to inputs using a parametric production function. The outputs are: gross hauled tonne-kilometres by freight trains; and gross hauled tonne-kilometres by passenger trains. The inputs are: engines and railcars; labour force; lines not electrified; and lines electrified. For more information, see Pestieau (1993), pp. 136-7.
Source: Pestieau (1993).

Table 29. **Efficiency decomposition into managerial and regulatory efficiency**

Railway		Autonomy per cent	Parametric frontier (DOLS[1])					
			Railway	Managerial efficiency	Railway	Regulatory efficiency	Railway	Gross efficiency
BLS	**Switzerland**	**100.0**	**TCDD**	**1.00000**	**BLS**	**1.00000**	**NS**	**0.87760**
BR	United Kingdom	76.3	NS	0.98374	SJ	0.93026	TCDD	0.84747
CFF	**Switzerland**	**66.0**	**VR**	**0.96726**	**BR**	**0.91609**	**BR**	**0.82139**
CFL	Luxembourg	63.5	CIE	0.95920	NS	0.89211	CFF	0.81208
CH	Greece	47.3	CFF	0.92910	SNCF	0.89005	CIE	0.80536
CIE	Ireland	58.3	SNCF	0.90452	FS	0.87832	SNCF	0.80506
CP	Portugal	64.0	BR	0.89662	CFF	0.87405	BLS	0.78772
DB	Germany	61.0	CP	0.88141	SNCB	0.86756	CP	0.76275
DSB	Denmark	41.5	RENFE	0.87924	CP	0.86538	SJ	0.72884
FS	Italy	67.0	OBB	0.86761	CFL	0.86318	VR	0.71881
NS	Netherlands	70.3	DB	0.80138	DB	0.85202	RENFE	0.71270
NSB	Norway	45.3	FS	0.79960	TCDD	0.84747	FS	0.70230
OBB	Austria	41.8	SNCB	0.79937	CIE	0.83962	SNCB	0.69350
RENFE	Spain	52.3	CH	0.79188	RENFE	0.81059	DB	0.68279
SJ	Sweden	80.0	BLS	0.78772	CH	0.78462	OBB	0.65402
SNCB	Belgium	64.5	SJ	0.78348	NSB	0.77372	CH	0.62133
SNCF	France	69.8	DSB	0.76652	OBB	0.75382	CFL	0.61912
TCDD	Turkey	60.0	NSB	0.73518	DSB	0.75206	DSB	0.67647
VR	Finland	40.0	CFL	0.71726	VR	0.74315	NSB	0.56882

1. Displaced ordinary least squares.
Source: Pestieau (1993).

The revision of the law on railways, accepted by Parliament in spring 1995, should pave the way for these reforms. The new law will facilitate the creation of markets in social services and will harmonise the principles governing the subsidies and the participation of the cantons in the financing of public transportation (CFF, PTT) and regional semi-private companies. The group of experts estimated that their reforms could effect for the Confederation substantial economies, mainly through better targeting of services and tighter cost control. Realised savings may, however, be less than hoped insofar as the experts may have adopted optimistic assumptions (from the Confederation's point of view) on the volume of non-commercial services to be performed.

The electricity industry

The electricity industry comprises firms engaged in the production, transportation and/or distribution of electricity. There are approximately 1 200 such firms in Switzerland, of which 1 000 are local utility companies primarily engaged in the distribution of electricity bought from larger companies. A few dozen middle-sized companies distribute, and sometimes, produce electricity at the urban, regional and cantonal levels. The six largest companies produce, transport and, to a lesser extent, distribute electricity at the regional level and handle all imports and exports.

The Swiss industry is largely publicly owned. In addition to those entities owned outright, the state (cantons and communes) owns 75 per cent of the shares in the private companies in this industry. Most utilities are controlled by the cantons and the communes, including the six major utilities; four of these are private companies in which the State holds 75 per cent of the shares. With a majority of the directors of these firms representing the cantons and the communes, political factors clearly play a significant role in the firms' decisions.[103]

Electricity production and distribution is subject to a regime of concessions.[104] In practice, this means that utilities enjoy a geographical monopoly which, however, is heavily regulated. Prices are administered and typically fixed at average total cost. Wide differences in costs and prices can be observed across the country.

Swiss electricity prices have fallen in real terms for most of the past twenty years, as have prices for most industrial products.[105] Since 1992, however, real prices have been increasing. Compared with other OECD countries, Swiss electricity prices in 1993 were moderate for households (Figure 22) but high for businesses (Figure 23). This structure of tariffs and the increases since 1992, a period of budgetary difficulties for cantons and communes, is suggestive of the importance of political as opposed to commercial factors in the management of this industry.

A recent federal government report[106] recommends far reaching reforms in this sector. The centre-piece of these proposals is to oblige owners of the transport and distribution network to sell access to third party generators; this is

Figure 22. **ELECTRICITY PRICES AND TAXES FOR HOUSEHOLDS, 1993[1]**

US cents/kWh

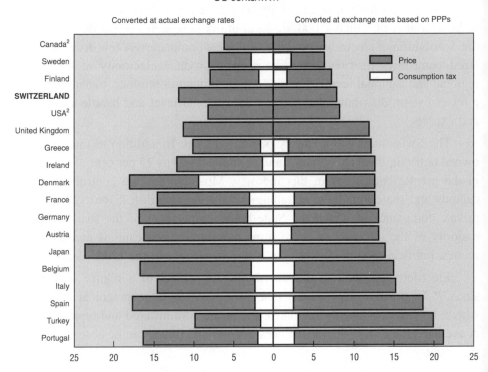

1. Average for the year.
2. No information concerning taxes.
Source: OECD, International Energy Agency.

Figure 23. **ELECTRICITY PRICES AND TAXES FOR INDUSTRY, 1993[1]**

US cents/kWh

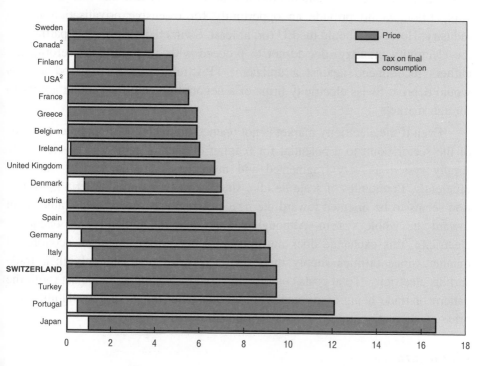

1. Average for the year.
2. No information concerning taxes.
Source: OECD, International Energy Agency.

known as "third party access" (TPA). This reform is along similar lines to that currently being considered by the EU. For such a proposal to be operational, it is recommended in the Swiss report that separate accounts be kept ("unbundling") for the generation, transport and distribution functions of vertically integrated enterprises. This reform would permit the natural monopoly part of the industry, the transport and distribution network, to be separated from the potentially competitive part, generation. With increased competition in the electricity industry, the report recommends that price control (in the wholesale market) could be removed; competition should then ensure that prices on the wholesale market better reflect marginal costs, permitting more rational use of existing and future production facilities. The authors of the report also consider that this increase in competition would provide an opportunity for extensive privatisation in the industry. However, should the EU (or, at least, Switzerland's principal partners in the electricity industry) decide not to proceed with a similar TPA reform, the authors recommend against a unilateral TPA reform in Switzerland as this would deprive Swiss electricity firms of a negotiating chip for gaining access to foreign markets.

Even if the electricity market is not opened up to competition, other features of the sector point to a potential for reaping efficiency gains.[107] The electricity supply system is very fragmented and investments are not carried out very efficiently. Economies of scale lie idle, since short-term and long-term optimisation seems to be oriented toward the needs of regional supply areas rather than toward the whole system. Although cantons and municipalities do exchange electricity, this exchange does not appear to be carried out in an economical manner, since utilities supply their own territories first and only then trade surplus electricity. Total costs could be lowered by trading at the outset (with the pattern of trade being associated with, among other things, the availability and price of alternative energy sources within the various regions).

Fire insurance

Fire insurance is provided in most cantons by state-owned companies which enjoy a legislated monopoly in their canton; only seven of the 26 cantons do not have such arrangements. This privileged position is reinforced by the fact that fire insurance is compulsory; it is optional in only three cantons, none of which has a monopoly fire insurance company. These companies were first created in the 19th century because the private mutual organisations which existed at the time were unable to insure against major fires.[108] Nowadays, the public insurance companies also offer cover against some natural disasters, including floods and avalanches, and some also offer cover against earthquakes, terrorist attacks and riots. Their other main activities are in the fields of fire prevention and fire fighting. The premiums charged by these companies only partly reflect the risks being insured as the principle of social solidarity amongst the insured is also taken into account. Premiums vary considerably between cantons.

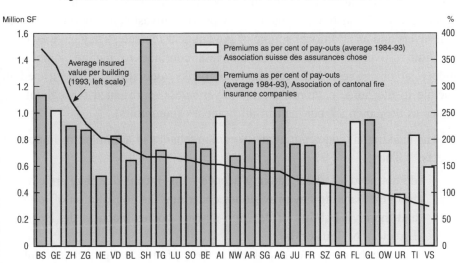

Figure 24. **PREMIUMS RELATIVE TO PAY-OUTS FOR FIRE INSURANCE**

Source: Schips, B., 1995.

The EEA negotiations and the trend towards deregulation in other countries have motivated a debate in Switzerland about the liberalisation of the market for fire insurance and the privatisation of the cantonal fire insurance companies.[109] However, the case for liberalisation is weakened by the fact that premia are lower in cantons with a public fire insurance company. This price advantage seems to be due mainly to the lower pay-outs which public companies have to make for fire damage.[110] Indeed, this price advantage is achieved in spite of a higher spread between payouts and premia[111] (Figure 24). On balance, the market should be liberalised only if the same low levels of fire damage and premia can be obtained through private insurance arrangements.[112]

Cantonal banks

Cantonal banks are those created by a cantonal statute and with liabilities guaranteed by the canton.[113] Although in legal terms the banks need not be owned by the cantons, they are in practice. Cantonal banks were mostly created in the 19th century to foster growth in the cantonal economy and to encourage home ownership by providing cheap credit respectively to local firms and to home buyers. The banks also were intended to provide investment opportunities for small savers and an additional source of government revenue. They have evolved since into universal banks but nevertheless continue to pursue some non-commercial objectives. Although cantonal banks' operations are restricted in principle to the home canton, they are nevertheless represented throughout the country as they own 27 per cent of all branches (comptoirs).

The banking law does not apply to cantonal banks in a number of important respects.[114] They:

-   do not need a federal banking licence – this means that they are exempt from the banking law provisions concerning the constitution of reserves and the civil liability of decision-making bodies (such as the Board of Directors or Trustees);
-   can only be created or dissolved by the canton – creditors cannot initiate bankruptcy proceedings;
-   are not automatically subject to the surveillance of the federal commission of banks.

The state guarantee on liabilities and the aforementioned exemptions from banking law are unlikely to have encouraged prudent practices.

Cantonal banks, of which there are 25, account for more than a third of savings deposits in Switzerland. This provides them with a relatively cheap source of finance. Despite their privileged position, they have lost market share, especially during the 1980s (Figure 25); their share of total banking assets fell from 36 per cent in 1955 to 21 per cent in 1993 and their share of the mortgage market fell from 50 per cent to 36 per cent over the same period. The productivity performance of cantonal banks has been poor compared to that of other banks in recent years,[115] owing in part to the restrictions on their activities and their inability fully to take advantage of the internationalisation of the financial industry.

Some cantonal banks have faced severe financial difficulties in recent years as a result of non-performing real-estate loans made during the late 1980s, when the property market was booming; as in other countries, many real-estate loans became unperforming as a result of the recession, falling real-estate prices and borrowers' frequently high gearing.[116] Although all banks have been affected by

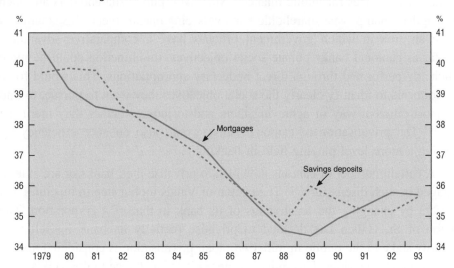

Figure 25. **MARKET SHARE OF THE CANTONAL BANKS**

Mortgages

Savings deposits

Source: Banque nationale suisse.

non-performing real-estate loans, this posed greater difficulties for cantonal (and regional)[117] banks as they had less reserves with which to absorb the losses.

Two cantonal banks – Solothurn[118] and Bern[119] – would have failed had it not been for cantonal rescue packages. In the case of Solothurn, this involved writing off the canton's interest (capital de dotation) in the bank (SF 170 million), privatising it[120] and sharing in certain future losses which potentially could amount to SF 1.4 billion.[121] In addition, the canton undertook to continue to guarantee time deposits up to their maturity and sight deposits until the end of 1996. With respect to Bern, the bank's non-performing and doubtful loans were transferred to a newly-created financial company (Dezennium Finanz AG). The total direct and indirect cost of these losses for the canton of Bern is estimated to amount to around SF 1 billion over the next ten years.

These developments have raised doubts about the wisdom of having cantonal banks. As some other countries also have found, the moral hazard problems associated with publicly-owned banks with deposit guarantees tend to encourage them to take larger- and/or less well-judged risks than private banks, with unfortunate consequences for public finances. Moreover, public shareholders are often less vigilant than private shareholders in overseeing management; this is unlikely to be an area in which government officials have a comparative advantage. Insofar as cantonal banks pursue social objectives, this function could be more efficiently performed through direct budgetary appropriations. This would force governments to identify clearly the social objectives they want to pursue, to find the most efficient way of achieving them and to judge whether they merit the cost.[122] The privatisation of cantonal banks would also enhance efficiency by creating a more level playing field in banking.

A certain number of cantons now plan to privatise their banks or are at least engaged in such discussions.[123] The canton of Valais took a step in this direction in 1993 by changing the legal status of its bank to that of a corporation. The canton of St. Gallen has decided to privatise partially its bank by selling a minority stake to the public in mid-1996; total privatisation is considered not yet to be politically feasible. This move has necessitated a change in the bank's legal structure which should increase its flexibility. The main aim of the partial privatisation is to share the bank's risk with the private sector. The canton will retain a majority stake in the bank and will maintain the deposit guarantee. The canton of Bern has also opted for a partial privatisation of its cantonal bank. The bank will be turned into a corporation[124] and, in 1998, less than half of its shares will be sold to the public. For the time being, there are no plans to privatise cantonal banks not in difficulty.[125]

Assessment

Switzerland's political institutions and democratic decision-making procedures – in particular the reliance on referenda – may ensure that decisions, once taken, have broad legitimacy, but often mean that decision making is slow. Within this framework of slow, consensual politics, the authorities have made progress in public sector reform. Some initiatives attempt to streamline and to improve the client focus of traditional government. The Federal government, through its efforts to improve management control in various administrative functions, has taken worthwhile initiatives. Likewise, cantonal and municipal governments have undertaken various reforms that may prove useful. These moves are to be commended; indeed, ongoing attempts to improve the efficiency and quality of public services and administration are, almost by definition, essential ingredients of effective government. Although these reforms have been stimulated, in part, by the increasing pressures felt by all levels of government to rein in growing deficits, it should be recognised that such reforms can only be part of the solution to this problem; addressing the burgeoning welfare expenditures would be an indispensable part of any durable solution to budgetary problems.

Other public sector reforms concern infrastructure management. These encompass the inter-connected areas of regulation, state-ownership and competition policy. Two sectors in particular – telecommunications and electricity – stand out as problem areas.

Telecommunications is a fast-moving sector in which developments do not appear to be waiting on the consensual nature of Swiss politics. Many of Switzerland's key economic partners have liberalised their telecommunications systems and many are likely to do so in the near future. Switzerland's reforms leave it with a system that is still very much protected from competitive pressures. This is beginning to show up in the quality and, especially, price of services. The quality of telecommunications services in Switzerland appears to be only average and customers have not reaped the full benefits of technological progress in the form of lower prices. Telecommunications prices charged in Switzerland have increased dramatically (relative to the OECD average) over the last four years. The cost of delaying reform in this area may be substantial. While telecommunications is a key enabling service for all economic sectors, its importance for other service industries is critical. Thus, top priority must be given to opening up the sector to all of the numerous forms that competition in telecommunications can now take.

The electrical power industry also presents opportunities for making important reforms. As noted, the electricity sector consists of local and regional monopolies serving exclusive supply areas.[126] The sheer number of utilities – 1 200 for a country as small as Switzerland – indicates that many of them are operating below the optimal size of a modern power company. Interventions from cantonal and municipal governments lack transparency and sometimes appear to distort prices. Moreover, prices appear to be based on average rather than marginal costs, as would be required for efficient resource allocation. Electricity companies enjoy a monopoly position due, among other things, to the exclusive supply franchises granted to them by the municipalities. The high degree of vertical integration between power generation and distribution parties precludes competition even in areas where such competition is technically feasible. Abolition of exclusive supply areas and monopolistic structures in the power market has been and remains an important topic in many member countries' energy debates. Whereas quite a number of countries have taken swift action, Switzerland has yet to make significant reforms.

IV. Conclusions

The Swiss economy registered positive growth in 1994 for the first time since 1990, led by a turnaround of fixed investment, accelerating exports and a strong build up of inventories. The rebound of domestic demand induced a surge of imports, but with a substantial terms-of-trade gain, the current external surplus declined only by 1 per cent of GDP to 7 per cent in 1994. In the spring of 1995, the Swiss franc strengthened further, and signs of a renewed weakening of growth emerged. Consumer confidence and a number of business survey indicators no longer seemed to be on a clear upward trend. Declining order inflows also pointed to decelerating construction investment this year, though this is in part due to the phasing out of the federal investment bonus programme. At the same time, wage moderation and increased social security contributions are likely to restrain the growth of private disposable incomes. All this contributes to the projected slowdown of growth this year.

A mild reacceleration in economic growth can, however, be expected for 1996. Government spending is set to remain constrained by ongoing efforts to reduce budget deficits. But, even though further market share losses are inevitable because of the stronger Swiss franc, exports are likely to remain a mainstay of activity, benefiting from vigorous export market growth in general and strengthening demand for investment goods in the OECD area in particular. Machinery and equipment investment should continue its brisk expansion as the back-log of demand has not yet been entirely eliminated, and because the abolition of the turnover tax on investment goods ("taxe occulte") with the introduction of VAT has increased the profitability of capital spending. Some pick up in private consumption and building activity should also be possible in 1996, when employment growth should boost household incomes and business capacity utilisation increases further.

One notable feature of the current recovery is that employment has responded to output growth with a longer lag than in previous upswings, having continued to fall until mid-1994. Another is the sharp increase in long-term unemployment, to 50 000 (30 per cent of total unemployment) in 1994 from only around 1 000 (under 7 per cent) in 1990. However, with the labour force contracting, largely on account of a falling labour participation rate, the seasonally adjusted unemployment rate fell, from its peak of 5 per cent at the beginning of 1994 to 4.2 per cent in May 1995. Part of the shrinking labour force is due to increased participation in education and training, often motivated by poor employment prospects. Also, some job seekers who have exhausted entitlements – currently after 400 days – might have chosen not to register any longer with the labour office, thereby dropping out of the labour force statistics.

Labour-market indicators suggest that the rate of so-called structural ("natural") unemployment has increased in Switzerland, estimates of which range from 1 to about 3½ per cent. The higher proportion of unemployment that cannot be expected to disappear simply as a result of output growth means that a stronger emphasis than hitherto should be placed on structural measures to combat unemployment, along the lines of those suggested in the OECD Jobs Study. The recent reform of unemployment insurance, making the receipt of insurance benefits after a certain period contingent upon participation in employment programmes or training schemes, is a step in the right direction.

Consumer price inflation, after having stood at 3½ per cent for nearly 1½ years, began to decline rapidly from late 1993 onward. It reached about ½ per cent in May 1994, where it remained for the rest of the year. The 1994 inflation rate of 0.9 per cent was the third lowest in the OECD and meant a broadly stable price level given the likely measurement bias in the consumer price index (CPI). With the replacement of the old turnover tax on goods by a general VAT at a slightly higher rate, CPI inflation jumped to 2.1 per cent in June 1995. So far, the increase in the price level has remained below "mechanical" estimates of the VAT-induced price effect on account of the strongly appreciating Swiss franc, moderate wage growth and the significant output gap, estimated by the OECD to be around 2 per cent or more at the beginning of 1995. With the effects of Swiss franc appreciation petering out but the output gap projected to remain broadly unchanged, CPI inflation will probably only rise a little in 1996.

The challenge facing the Swiss National Bank (SNB) now is to preserve price stability while supplying enough central bank money for a fuller utilisation of human and physical resources. The SNB has in principle accommodated the higher level of demand for money in the economy entailed by the introduction of the VAT. But all available evidence indicates that, more generally, the SNB has erred on the side of caution. Various indicators suggest that monetary conditions are tight at the current juncture: the growth of broader monetary aggregates such as M1 has slowed down, the effective Swiss franc exchange rate has appreciated by a substantial amount and real short- and long-term interest rates are still high for the early phase of an upswing. Measures of the output gap suggest that the economy could grow faster without risking accelerating inflation. All these elements suggest that, if these conditions persist, further monetary easing would be appropriate.

But striking the right balance between monetary firmness to keep the price level broadly stable and adequately supporting economic activity has become more difficult than in the previous decade. This is due to the emergence of considerable uncertainties about how to interpret movements of the adjusted monetary base, the SNB's intermediate monetary target and preferred indicator of monetary conditions, in an environment of technological and legal change. Several shifts in the demand for base money during the first five-year target period from 1990 to 1994 were acknowledged by the SNB when it set the starting point of the new target line below the end point of the previous one. In view of possible further instability of demand for base money, the role of other indicators should be upgraded. Broader monetary aggregates, in particular M1, which clearly represented monetary conditions better than base money immediately after the legal and technical changes of 1988, ought to be given a more prominent role as indicators of monetary conditions. The concomitant de-emphasising of the monetary base as an intermediate target would guard against the potentially adverse effects on the SNB's credibility that repeated failure to meet the target might have. To increase transparency, other indicators such as the exchange rate, the output gap and wage settlements, which the SNB closely monitors anyway, should be taken into account more explicitly in monetary policy decisions and announcements.

Government finances improved in 1994 for the first time in almost a decade, with the deficit on the consolidated account of the general government and social security falling to 3.1 per cent of GDP. Much of the decline reflected an improvement in the financial position of the unemployment insurance fund and the strong revenue growth in an even-numbered year associated with the biennial system for collecting the federal income tax. No further improvement is projected in 1995, leaving the cyclically-adjusted deficit of the general government at an estimated 1.7 per cent of GDP. This structural deficit is mainly attributable to the Confederation and, to a lesser extent, the cantons.

The Confederation aims to reduce its debt as a proportion of GDP in the medium term and to this end proposed a consolidation programme (*troisième programme d'assainissement*) to eliminate the structural deficit by 1998. However, Parliament rejected virtually all of the proposed revenue measures. Adjusting the Finance Plan for this decision implies a projected reduction in the deficit to SF 4 billion (1 per cent of GDP) in 1998, of which half is estimated to be structural. In view of the medium-term budgetary outlook, which has since deteriorated, additional budgetary consolidation clearly will be required to achieve the Confederation's fiscal objectives and to provide greater room for manœuvre in the next cyclical downturn.

Governments in Switzerland have, in recent decades, sought to curb the seemingly incessant pressure for higher government expenditure with direct controls, such as freezes on government employment and/or government wages and requirements for qualified parliamentary majorities to approve new expenditure programmes. As in other countries, these measures have had largely disappointing results. The need to achieve fiscal consolidation at all levels of government in Switzerland in recent years has awakened an interest in more profound reforms in the public sector aimed at increasing efficiency, although these could only partially alleviate expenditure pressures as they relate for the most part to growing social entitlements. The interest in reform has been sharpened by pressure from users of public-sector services, especially business, for better value services. Users are demanding to be treated as clients, to receive services well adapted to their requirements and priced competitively. There is a growing realisation in Switzerland, as in other OECD countries, that improving the quality of public-sector services and the efficiency with which they are delivered requires fundamental reforms.

The agenda for such reforms which is developing in Switzerland and in other OECD countries is inspired by private-sector practice. The new framework, known as New Public Management (NPM), typically involves separation of political and administrative functions, delegation of non-political decision-making powers to administrative managers accompanied by enhanced accountability and control systems, and greater use of contracting out in areas where feasible. Partial moves along these lines are evident in some aspects of government reform in Switzerland, but the reform process is not as advanced as in some other countries.

Initiatives have been implemented or proposed at all levels of government. For example, the federal government proposes to strengthen the policy-making branch of government and to identify more clearly the objectives to be pursued by the administrative parts of government. Moreover, the federal government recently announced its intention to give certain offices a mandate specifying the services to be supplied and a multi-year budget. The widespread use of contracting out by lower levels of government also has the potential to enhance efficiency, although this potential is often unrealised due to the uncompetitive conditions under which contracts frequently are awarded. But in other respects, it is some of the cantons which have gone farthest in administrative reform. The canton of Valais has re-examined its whole administration and is now planning to implement measures which will significantly reduce public employment. The canton of Bern also is currently preparing a reform package to introduce NPM practices. And the city of Bern has launched a number of pilot projects in which services have been completely reorganised along NPM principles, including monitoring user satisfaction with the relevant services; Lucerne plans similar projects. If experience in other OECD countries with similar reforms is a useful guide, these reforms should deliver encouraging results. There is certainly scope to extend such reforms in Switzerland, including at the federal level of government.

Reforms are also being introduced in Switzerland's government business enterprises which, as in most other European countries, dominate infrastructure industries. Non-commercial services are being more clearly identified and increasingly subsidised directly instead of through cross subsidies from profitable business activities; such reforms have been most significant at the PTT. Reforms are also planned to give managers greater autonomy in deciding how to achieve their objectives, including authority for decisions on financial and personnel (including remuneration) matters; the "TOP" project for reorganising the PTT

111

currently under discussion is perhaps the most far reaching in this regard. There have also been some moves to allow competition in areas formerly reserved for public monopolies, such as the recent liberalisation of the market for end-user telecommunications equipment and for service provision (with the exception of voice telephony). Full reform of this sector must be vigorously pursued if the unfavourable movements of Swiss telecommunications prices observed during the last five years (relative to those prevailing in countries with more competitive telecommunications systems) are to be reversed.

These reforms are motivated by the desire not only to improve efficiency, but also to ensure that Switzerland's regulatory framework is Euro-compatible. And the EU is currently considering substantial reforms in the regulatory framework for infrastructure industries which were formerly considered to be natural monopolies. The essence of these reforms, which affect in particular the telecommunications and electricity industries, is to separate their natural monopoly from their potentially competitive parts and to provide a regulatory framework which supports competition where feasible. This requires regulations which provide for third party access to distribution networks (such as power lines, telephone cables and microwave frequencies) at efficient prices. The reforms to date at the PTT, in particular, have been designed to prepare it for greater competition in the future. But the reforms envisaged by the EU would, if followed in Switzerland, lead to a considerable increase in competition in the telecommunications and electricity industries. Given the importance of these industries in modern economies, the Swiss authorities should endeavour to move with the EU on these reforms.

Although public ownership of business enterprises is generally limited to infrastructure industries, there are a few exceptions, notably the cantonal banks, whose liabilities are guaranteed by the government, and the cantonal fire insurance companies. As the reasons for which these banks were created no longer hold and owning them is unlikely to be an efficient way of achieving whatever social objectives are now assigned to them, they should be privatised. On the other hand, liberalisation of cantonal fire insurance companies would be unlikely to improve efficiency.

In conclusion, the Swiss economy now has achieved price stability, and output and employment have been brought back on an upward trend after a long and painful recession. Important progress in structural reform has been made recently with the introduction of VAT and amendments to the occupational pension system, which will enhance the mobility of labour. In other reform areas progress has seemed tortoise-like, compared with the experience in other OECD countries. However, progress has picked up in recent weeks, with the lower House of Parliament passing legislation on key areas of the federal government's revitalisation package, including the deregulation of the domestic market, liberalisation of public procurement and the reform of competition law. Full implementation of the reforms envisaged would contribute to a higher growth potential and the maintenance of price stability.

Notes

1. This figure is derived from a quarterly output-based GDP series estimated by the *Office fédéral des questions conjoncturelles*. The *Office fédéral* also makes estimates of all expenditure components except stockbuilding. Inventory accumulation (including errors and omissions) is then calculated as the difference between output-based GDP and the sum of the estimated final expenditure components and net exports. According to the preliminary figures of the *Office fédéral*, stockbuilding accounts for 1.7 percentage points of the rate of growth of GDP in 1994. However, the Konjunkturforschungsstelle (KOF) in Zürich challenges the estimates of the *Office fédéral*. On the basis of their business surveys, the KOF arrives at a contribution of stockbuilding to GDP growth of 1.4 percentage points. In addition, the KOF also estimates lower growth of construction investment ($3^3/_4$ instead of $4^1/_2$ per cent) and government consumption ($^1/_2$ instead of $1^1/_2$ per cent) than the *Office fédéral*. Altogether the KOF arrives at an average GDP growth rate of only 1.5 per cent in 1994. Unless otherwise indicated, this *Survey* uses the estimates of the *Office fédéral*.

2. See also the comparison of Swiss business cycles in the 1992-93 OECD *Economic Survey of Switzerland*, Chapter II.

3. Of the four available construction cost indices, those of Zurich, Bern and Lucerne fell in 1992-93. In 1994, a further decline was registered in Zurich, while Bern and Lucerne recorded increases. Construction costs were on a rising trend in Geneva in 1993-94, after three years of decline.

4. An official breakdown of total construction investment into components is not yet available for 1994.

5. However, since the bonuses are to be paid after the completion of the projects, most of the payments will be effected only in 1995. If all projects under the programme had indeed been additional, then the SF 200 million spent for the 15 per cent bonus would have created extra orders of around SF 1 200 million, or some $2^1/_4$ per cent of annual construction in current prices (about $^1/_3$ per cent of nominal GDP).

6. The rise in household direct taxes by about 7 per cent in 1994 is primarily an effect of the peculiar Swiss tax system, which makes direct tax payments grow strongly in even years and weaken in odd years (see Chapter II below).

7. Sectoral value-added figures are estimates of the KOF (Zürich).

8. After the initial draft of this section had been prepared, the Office fédéral de la statistique (OFS) published results of its revision of the methodological basis of the labour

force statistics (see "La statistique de la population active occupée, Résultats révisés 1985-1995", Actualités OFS, Bern, June 1995). Because the full details of this revision were not available when this Survey was drafted, this section uses the earlier labour force statistics of the OFS and the quarterly data (number of jobs occupied) based on them published in KOF, Konjunktur, June 1995. Nevertheless, information on the OFS revised statistics has been added in several footnotes.

9. This time the lag was four quarters while in the recoveries beginning in 1976 and in 1983 it was only two quarters.

10. The OFS revised statistics suggest an average decrease in total employment by 0.3 per cent (12 000 persons) in 1994.

11. Industrial employment stagnated in 1994 according to the OFS revised statistics.

12. Industrial production (excluding hydroelectric power and electric and gas utilities) even increased by 7.9 per cent in 1994.

13. According to the revised statistics, total employment peaked at 3.866 million persons in 1991, some 300 000 higher than the old statistics. The revised statistics show a fall in employment from 1991 to 1994 of 2.4 per cent until 1994, equivalent to the cumulative loss of 94 000 jobs.

14. The revised statistics suggest that employment in manufacturing industries fell by 12¼ per cent – or some 100 000 jobs – between 1990 and 1993. Stagnating average industrial employment has been reported for 1994.

15. The revised labour force statistics report an increase in employment in services of 26 000 jobs (1 per cent) between 1991 and 1993 and stagnation in 1994.

16. The OFS revisions suggest that female employment was barely affected by the recession (–1.9 per cent between 1991 and 1993) while employment of men fell by 3.9 per cent from 1991 to 1994.

17. The revised statistics report a decline in employment of foreigners from 1.020 million in 1991 to 0.965 million in 1994 (a cumulative –5.4 per cent).

18. Not all of the persons who reach benefit termination – some 40 000 during 1994 – become hidden unemployed. It is estimated by the *Office fédéral de l'industrie, des arts et métiers et du travail* that currently about 20 per cent of the "exhaustees" find a job, 30 per cent remain registered as unemployed and the remainder falls out of the statistics. Of these remaining 50 per cent, some may have found a job or continue to seek one without the assistance of the labour office, some take up training, some leave the country and some withdraw from the labour force.

19. However, the revised OFS statistics recorded a marginal increase (+0.1 per cent) in Swiss nationals' employment while that of foreigners fell by 1.6 per cent in 1994.

20. This is a comparison of actual output with a long-term log-linear trend. Starting after the very severe recession of the mid-1970s, the (constant) slope of a log-linear trend line equals 2 per cent.

21. Potential output proxied by the low-frequency component of real GDP applying a Hodrick-Prescott filter.

22. *Cf.* Edey (1994).

23. A federal decree authorises an increase of rents by 2 to 3 per cent for each quarter of a percentage point increase in the mortgage rate, depending on the actual level of the mortgage rate. With a weight of 22 per cent in the consumer price index (CPI), the impact of rents on general consumer price inflation is substantial. The discontinuous effect of housing rent changes on the CPI stems from their being recorded every three months only (February, May, August and November).

24. However, it has also been observed that administered prices exert a stabilising effect in periods of accelerating inflation.

25. Neither producer nor import prices are *directly* affected by the transition to VAT. However, the abolition of the taxation of production inputs has a cost-dampening effect which could gradually reduce producer prices by up to ¾ per cent in 1995 according to KOF estimates.

26. Under the old turnover tax regime, building work was taxed at three-quarters of the standard rate of 6.2 per cent, hence 4.65 per cent.

27. The conspicuously divergent movement of rents and the price of services less rents at the beginning of 1995 as shown in the third panel of Figure 7 is due to the exemption of housing rents from VAT.

28. This estimate is derived from the employment series published in KOF, *Konjunktur,* June 1995. When using the revised OFS labour force statistics, the gain in the total economy's labour productivity amounts to 2.4 per cent in 1994, hence still around 1 percentage point above the estimated nominal wage increase.

29. These figures are still provisional. Indeed, latest information suggests that net investment income may have been higher both in 1993 and 1994 than initially estimated. This may result in an upward revision of the current external surplus in both years, possibly to 8.4 per cent of GDP in 1993 and to 7.8 per cent in 1994.

30. The seasonally-adjusted monetary base comprises notes in circulation and sight deposits held with the National Bank. In addition to its seasonal adjustment, the series is corrected for the biennial peak in note circulation at the end of even years, when property and income taxes are assessed, because of evidence that taxpayers try to lower their tax base by converting parts of their financial assets into currency.

31. *Cf.* "La politique monétaire suisse en 1994", *Monnaie et conjoncture*, Bulletin trimestriel de la Banque nationale suisse, décembre 1993, p. 261.

32. As measured by an index of trade-weighted relative consumer prices in a common currency.

33. Applying ordinary least squares regression analysis, the single-equation model seeks to explain the change in the Confederation bond rate by the change in the German long-term bond rate, the ratio of the current external balance to GDP, the change in the Swiss short-term interest rate, the Swiss-German inflation differential and the Swiss-German growth differential. The estimation results and test statistics are presented in footnote 26 and the tracking performance is shown in Diagram 15 of the 1994 OECD *Economic Survey of Switzerland.*

34. The average real bond rate as derived from the filtered GDP deflator was 1¾ per cent in 1993 and 2¾ per cent in 1994, whereas it was only ½ per cent in 1983 and 1 per cent

in 1977. About the same holds for the (*ex post*) real three-month Euro-Swiss franc rate which was between ³/₄ and 1 per cent in 1977 and in 1983, but at 2³/₄ per cent in 1994.

35. The exact base period of the targeting exercise was made public only in December 1992, hence two years after the change in its general approach had been announced by the National Bank. *Cf.* "La politique monétaire suisse en 1993", *Monnaie et conjoncture,* Bulletin trimestriel de la Banque nationale suisse, décembre 1992.

36. *Cf.* "La politique monétaire suisse en 1995", *Monnaie et conjoncture,* Bulletin trimestriel de la Banque nationale suisse, décembre 1994, p. 267.

37. *Ibid.,* p. 272.

38. *Ibid.*

39. *Ibid.,* p. 267. Earlier SNB publications defined "price stability" as CPI inflation in the 0 to 1 per cent range. *Cf.,* for example, Rich (1992), p. 73, or Fischer and Zurlinden (1994), p. 72. In a recent meeting of the General Assembly of the SNB, Chairman of the Board Lusser defined CPI inflation between 1 and 2 per cent as consistent with price stability. See the box in the *Neue Zürcher Zeitung* of 22/23 April 1995, p. 9.

40. This is roughly in line with average velocity growth during the past four years, but below the long-term trend growth of income velocity of base money.

41. "... there is no longer any doubt that the demand for money has decreased permanently." (*Monnaie et conjoncture,* décembre 1994, *op. cit.,* p. 273). The SNB thereby acknowledges earlier criticism that adopting a new money supply rule as early as 1990, shortly after the innovation of 1988, was premature as a new equilibrium relationship between the demand for base money and its major macroeconomic determinants variables – real growth, prices and interest rates – had not yet re-established itself (see Chapters II of the 1993 and 1994 OECD *Economic Surveys of Switzerland*). The Bank does not make explicit how it quantified the magnitude of the structural shift in the demand for base money.

42. Before 1995 the sight-deposit component of base money also covered National Bank deposits of a few institutions which were neither banks nor finance companies. From 1995 on these institutions' sight deposits, which amount to some SF 100 million, are no longer included in the monetary base.

43. These problems have been discussed in earlier *Surveys.* See, for example, the 1987/88 OECD *Economic Survey of Switzerland,* Chapter II.

44. See also Peytrignet (1995).

45. The deficit referred to here and subsequently is measured using the definitions in the *Statistique Financière Révisée* (SFR), unless otherwise indicated. Use of this definition makes the Confederation accounts comparable with those of the cantons and communes. The major adjustment required to convert the Confederation's financial accounts to a SFR basis is to exclude the notional payments to the Confederation associated with the investment of the Confederation's interest payments and contributions to the Federal Insurance Fund (*Caisse fédérale d'assurance*); this fund provides the "second pillar" part of Confederation employees' retirement pensions.

46. Financial accounts basis.

47. The data discussed in this subsection are on a financial account basis.

48. These loans declined by SF 0.9 billion to SF 1.15 billion. They are included in the "interest, loans, acquisition of holdings" row in Table 13.

49. Income for the federal income tax is assessed and, with a one year lag, paid over two-year periods. For example, taxes paid in 1994-95 relate to income assessed for 1991-92. This system gives rise to stronger revenue growth in even-numbered years than in odd-numbered years.

50. These loans were SF ¾ billion less than budgeted.

51. The CFA is the "second pillar" pension scheme for federal government employees.

52. These budget projections are based on the Federal Government's projections of 1.5 per cent real growth and 2½ per cent inflation in 1995.

53. Budgeted payments to the unemployment insurance fund were SF 1.9 billion (a loan) in 1994 and SF 0.4 billion (a loan of SF 244 million and a transfer of SF 166 million) in 1995.

54. These payments appear in the "Loans and equity" row of Table 14.

55. In addition, magistrates and senior civil servants are to have a one-off pay cut and cost of living allowances for Zurich and Geneva are to be abolished.

56. These transfers are projected to grow by 10 per cent. They are included in the row "Contributions to current expenditures" in Table 14.

57. Nominal GDP is projected to grow by 4 per cent in 1995.

58. This effect can be seen in Table 15 in the negative growth projected for the federal income tax and for withholding tax on capital income ("impôt anticipé"). Although the gross proceeds from withholding tax are not affected by the biennial system for the federal income tax, refunds, and hence net proceeds from the withholding tax are affected; "Withholding tax" in Table 15 refers to net proceeds from withholding tax.

59. VAT is paid to the Government with a one quarter lag.

60. This and the following paragraph draw heavily on Witschard (1995).

61. The cyclically-adjusted budget balances discussed in this section were provided by the "Office Fédéral des Questions Conjoncturelles". The methodology used to make these calculations is described in Ammann (1995). Data have been adjusted for the lags between the accrual of incomes and their taxation, which differ between the Confederation and cantons as well as between cantons. In addition, loans made to the unemployment insurance fund by the Confederation and cantons are classified as cyclical expenditures. The potential growth rates underlying the estimates are 2.1 per cent for the period 1981 to 1989 and 1.7 per cent thereafter.

62. The data discussed in this subsection are on a financial accounts basis.

63. Some of the most important measures in the 1992 programme ("premier programme d'assainissement"), which reduced structural deficits in the medium-term by SF 3-4 billion, were a straight-line reduction in federal subsidies and loans (SF 800 million annual saving by 1995), an increase in petrol tax by 20 centimes per litre and an increase in tobacco taxes. With respect to the 1993 programme ("deuxième programme d'assainissement"), the most important measure was the shift to VAT from 1 January 1995, which was estimated to

generate an additional SF 1.6 billion in tax receipts by 1996; as VAT is paid after each quarter, this is the first year in which there will be a full year's receipts. A brake on expenditures was also proposed in the 1993 programme, according to which all parliamentary decisions resulting in increased expenditure above certain limits must be approved by a majority of all the members of both houses of Parliament; this measure, which is not expected to have a significant impact on the growth of expenditures, was approved in a referendum in March 1995.

64. In the case of the reform of company tax, Parliament indicated that the Federal Council should revise the proposition to make it acceptable, essentially by proposing a lower rate.

65. The data discussed in this subsection are on a financial account basis.

66. The extra expenditures associated with the restructuring of the railways (CFF), which involves significant management reforms (see Chapter III), are not taken into account.

67. Companies are subject to annual income taxation for 1995 and subsequent tax years.

68. Refunds in 1995, 1996-97, and 1998 will be based respectively on dividend and interest earnings in 1991-92, 1993-94, and 1995-96. Such earnings are likely to have been the highest in the first of these periods.

69. These include: the 9th revision of the old-age insurance scheme (AVS) in 1982, which increased the Confederation's contribution and introduced a mixed wage and price index for indexation purposes; in 1990, the subsidisation of sickness funds and the provision of assistance to refugees; and in 1991, an increase in age pensions to celebrate Switzerland's 700th anniversary.

70. Competition policy was examined at some length in the 1992 OECD *Economic Survey of Switzerland,* while the impacts of both regulation and competition policy on the housing and construction sectors were explored in the 1994 *Survey.*

71. Current as opposed to total general government outlays are discussed because investment data are not available on a general government basis in Switzerland. Nonetheless, investment expenditures by all levels of government are likely to amount to around 6 per cent of GDP.

72. The system was established in 1948. Increased expenditures associated with the maturing of the system mostly relate to old-age pensions.

73. Social welfare expenditure increased by 4 percentage points of GDP between 1990 and 1993.

74. This estimate is based on 1991 census data.

75. See Jans, A. and R. Meili (1988).

76. For example, the cut in federal subsidies for sickness insurance did not represent a saving for households, which were faced with increased premiums.

77. This study, which is to be ongoing, is carried out by the federal office of personnel. Other evaluations are carried out by research projects financed by the Swiss National Fund for Scientific Research.

78. This kind of reform has been taken farthest in the United Kingdom and New Zealand.

79. As this proposal was made in response to a request from Parliament, there is a good chance that there will be sufficient support in Parliament to pass the changes in law required to put the reform into effect; the laws concerned are on finance and on the measures to improve public finances. These laws are, however, subject to a faculatitive referendum.

80. This has been developed in collaboration with specialists at the University of St. Gallen. Inspiration for these reforms came in part from the experience of Tilburg, a Dutch city which dramatically turned its finances around by adopting NPM practices (Journal de Genève, 19 December 1994). There has been considerable interest in Swiss local government circles about NPM, as reflected in a series of articles last winter in the Journal de Genève.

81. The same could be said of reforms in these industries in many other European countries.

82. This assumption is challenged in the "theory of public choice", according to which behaviour in the public sector is influenced by incentives, as in the private sector. The assumption of a benevolent government, which underlay earlier economic analysis, was considered to be unreasonable.

83. Even without monopoly power, public ownership creates potential rents for management and employees by protecting them from the threats of take-over and bankruptcy.

84. The following description of the law on price surveillance is based on *Surveillance des prix: Rapport annuel 1991*. The relevant legislation is the law on price surveillance (*Loi sur le surveillance des prix*), which was passed by Parliament in 1991.

85. The loss for *La Poste* in 1994 (SF 146 million) is nevertheless a significant improvement compared with the early 1990's; the loss reached SF 800 million in 1991. This reduction in the loss was achieved by increasing prices for postal services and by implementing an extensive rationalisation programme ("maîtrise des coûts").

86. These amounted to 61 per cent of assets employed in 1993. The average interest rate paid by the PTT on its liabilities in 1993 was 1.2 per cent.

87. Following the creation of the new Federal Office for Communications, the telecommunications division has particular responsability for the liberalisation of the telecommunications market.

88. Reforms to this end also had to satisfy two major constraints: that they maintained the legal status of PTT as a public company; and that they safeguarded the unity of its services.

89. Article 36 of the Federal Constitution states that:
    i)   postal and telegraph services are a federal responsibility throughout Switzerland;
    ii) the revenues of postal and telegraph services belong to the federal treasury;
    iii) tariffs are to be fixed using the same principles and as fairly as possible throughout Switzerland.

90. This is required under Article 10 al 1 of the law on postal services (Loi sur le service de poste).

91. Payments to contractors offering these services were SF 220 million in 1993.

92. A recent survey confirms the importance of telecommunication services for internationalised firms. According to this survey, telecommunication infrastructure is the most important

domestic factor which determines internationalisation of export-oriented SMEs. See Dembinski, P. and H. Unterlerchner (1994).

93. This might, however, change in the future, especially since the EU has agreed to the liberalisation of infrastructure and reserved services from 1998.

94. The lower international tariffs may reflect a bias in the data in favour of OECD countries with close neighbours and the effects of pressure from business in Switzerland for lower international charges. Domestic services continue to be subsidised by international services in most OECD countries.

95. Shareholders include the Confederation, cantons, communes and private entities.

96. The CFF is much larger than the regional companies – in 1993, it transported 270 million passengers on a network of 2 980 kilometres, compared with the combined total for all 57 private railways of 110 million passengers on a network of 2 030 kilometres.

97. The same regulations apply to all railway companies. The companies need a federal concession to operate, which gives them a regional monopoly. They are obliged to provide regular services, according to an official timetable, and to apply an approved tariff schedule. The Confederation subsidises prices in alpine and peripheral areas as well as services in the public interest. Deficits are usually covered by the state, investment is financed by the Confederation and the cantons (by the Confederation for the CFF), the latter having no say on regulations.

98. In 1993, the Confederation paid the CFF SF 0.8 billion and regional companieswel SF 80 million for operating unprofitable services in the public interest. The Confederation also paid regional companies SF 130 million so that they could match CFF tariffs.

99. This project involves the construction of two tunnels through the Alps and the creation of related infrastructure to transport freight and truck traffic by rail. See 1994 OECD *Economic Survey of Switzerland,* Chapter III, for more details.

100. Efficiency is defined in terms of outputs relative to inputs. The outputs are: gross hauled tonne-kilometres by freight trains; and gross hauled tonne-kilometres by passenger trains. The inputs are: engines and railcars; labour force; lines not electrified; and lines electrified. For more information about this measure of efficiency, see Pestieau (1993), pp. 136-7.

101. Pestieau (1993), p. 140.

102. Interestingly, given the very complex shareholder structure and the dense regulation, owner-ship does not seem to influence cost efficiency. However, cost efficiency is positively related to the degree the cantons subsidise investment, but negatively to the way in which tariff subsidies are distributed. The authors of these findings conclude that the issue of the public or private ownership is probably of less relevance than questions related to the distribution of tasks and subsidies. Moreover, the private companies are mostly far from operating at an optimal scale and density. See for further details Filippini, M. and R. Maggi (1993).

103. Office fédéral de l'énergie (1995), (Cattin group report).

104. As are natural gas distribution and district heating (chauffage à distance).

105. Office fédéral de l'énergie (1995), (Cattin group report), p. 52.

106. *Ibid.*

107. This evaluation of the scope for rationalisation of the electrical power industry appears in the International Energy Agency's 1995 Review of Switzerland.

108. The canton of Aargau created the first public-fire insurance company in Switzerland in 1805. Other cantons quickly followed this example.

109. Private insurance companies favour liberalisation and have commissioned an expert report (B. Schips, 1995) in support of their case; R. Leu, A. Gemperle, M. Haas and S. Spycher (1993) also argues against the monopoly. Public insurance companies tend to oppose liberalisation and similarly have commissioned a report (Th. von Ungern-Sternberg, 1994) which supports their position.

110. See figure on p. 24, in B. Schips (1995), *op. cit.*

111. This suggests that administration costs and/or profit margins are higher for public companies than for private companies; public companies' large reserves may be indicative of high profit margins.

112. It is possible that the advantage of public fire insurance may stem from the fact that all incentives for effective fire prevention and fighting are focused on the same (public) entity. If these services are badly organised, the canton bears the cost through its fire insurance company, rather than shifting it to private insurers.

113. Article 31, Federal Constitution. Most (20 out of 25) cantonal banks have the legal form of an autonomous public establishment, with the others being corporations subject to a special law. The guarantee on liabilities is limited in the cases of the cantonal banks of Geneva and Vaud to savings deposits.

114. This special treatment arose following the cantonal banks' opposition to the revision of the banking law in 1933.

115. Sheldon (1994) found that for the period 1988-91, only regional banks recorded lower productivity growth.

116. Mortgages were granted for up to 100 per cent (and in some cases, even more) of property values at this time.

117. Regional banks were hit particularly hard by non-performing real-estate loans. As a result, many of these banks were forced to merge with larger banks; their number declined from 190 in 1989 to 138 in 1993. The bankruptcy of the regional Spar- und Leihkasse Thun in 1991 showed that the public could potentially lose part of their (savings) deposits.

118. An important cause of the Solothurn bank's difficulties was the bad financial situation of a smaller regional bank it took over.

119. A special factor contributing to the Bern bank's difficulties was bad loans to a speculator – Werner K. Rey – who since has fled the country and now is sought by the Swiss authorities.

120. Privatisation required a constitutional amendment, which was approved in a referendum. The bank was transformed into a corporation and sold to Swiss Bank Corporation, one of the Switzerland's four largest banks. Privatisation was considered to be the best way of limiting the canton's losses.

121. To cover these potential losses, provisions for bad debts were made in 1994 amounting SF 0.4 billion.

122. In making this assessment, the efficiency costs of distorting economic decisions should also be taken into account.

123. The canton of Aargau is willing to study a change in the legal status of its bank and to re-examine the issue of the deposit guarantee.

124. The proposed conversion of the bank into a corporation does not require a constitutional amendment. The cantonal constitution stipulates that the cantonal bank "encourages the economic and social development and helps the canton to carry out its tasks".

125. For example, the canton of Lucerne decided not to privatise its bank. The government stresses the usefulness of the services rendered by the bank to the region but has not totally discounted the idea of a partial privatisation in the future.

126. This assessment is taken from the International Energy Agency's 1995 Review of Switzerland.

References

Ammann (1995), *Le budget de plein emploi – un réexamen,* Office fédéral des questions conjoncturelles, étude No. 20, Bern.

Benninghoff, M. and P. Knoepfel (1994), "Le partenariat public-privé dans la politique des déchets", Cahiers de l'IDHEAP, No. 124, IDHEAP, Lausanne, March.

Blankart, Ch. (1977), Wohlfahrtsökonomie und Defizite öffentlicher Unternehmen: Das Beispiel der Bundesbahnen, *Revue suisse d'économie politique et statistique,* December.

Burgat, P. and Cl. Jeanrenaud (1990), "Mesure de l'efficacité productive et de l'efficacité de coût: cas des déchets ménagers en Suisse", IRER Working Papers No. 9002, Université de Neuchâtel, February.

Burgat, P. and Cl. Jeanrenaud (1992), "Measurement of productive efficiency: The example of household waste in Switzerland", IRER Working Papers No. 9209, University of Neuchâtel, September.

Commission suisse des cartels et du préposé à la surveillance des prix (1991), *Rapport annuel.*

Commission suisse des cartels et du préposé à la surveillance des prix (1995), *État de la concurrrence sur certains marchés des déchets,* No. 2/1995.

Conseil fédéral (1995), *Statut des banques cantonales, en particulier de la limitation de la responsabilité de l'État et privatisation,* Bern, March.

Dembinski, P. and H. Unterlerchner (1994), "L'internationalisation des PME suisses à l'horizon de l'an 2000", Georg, Geneva.

Direction générale des CFF (1994), *Rapport de gestion des Chemin de fers fédéraux – 1993,* Bern.

Direction générale des PTT (1994), *Rapport de gestion de l'entreprise des PTT – 1993,* Bern.

Edey, Malcolm (1994), "Costs and benefits of moving from low inflation to price stability", *OECD Economic Studies,* No. 23, Winter.

Elmeskow, Jorgen (1993), "High and persistent unemployment: Assessment of the problem and its causes", *OECD Economics Department Working Paper,* No. 132.

EPAC (1992), *Profitability and productivity of government business enterprises,* Research Paper No. 2, Canberra.

Ettlin, F. (1989), "Der schweizerische Notenumlauf 1962-1988: Eine ökonometrische Untersuchung aufgrund des Cointegrations- und Fehler-Korrektur-Ansatzes", *Monnaie et conjoncture,* Bulletin trimestriel de la Banque nationale suisse, September.

Fischer, Andreas M., and Zurlinden (1994), Mathias, "Geldpolitik mit formellen Inflationszielen: eine Übersicht", *Monnaie et conjuncture,* Bulletin trimestriel de la Banque nationale suisse, March.

Filippini, M. and R. Maggi (1993), "Efficiency and Regulation in the Case of the Swiss Private Railways", *Journal of Regulatory Economics,* Vol. 2, pp. 199-216.

Filippini, M. (1994), "Economies of scale and overcapitalisation in the Swiss electric power distribution industry", Institute for Empirical Research, Université de Zurich, May.

Fluri, R. (1995), "Grundlagen zur Revision der Geldaggregate im Jahre 1995", *Monnaie et conjoncture,* Bulletin trimestriel de la Banque nationale suisse, March.

Hansen, Chr. and B. Gorsler (1994), "Strukturen und Perspektiven des Elektrizitätsmarktes Schweiz", Brugger, Hansen und Partner, Zurich, January.

Huber-Berninger, M. and R. Hediger (1994), "Finanzierungssysteme zur privatwirtschaftlichen Verwertung und Behandlung von Abfällen", Schweizerischen Interessengemeinschaft für Abfallverminderung und der Aktion Saubere Schweiz (SIGA/ASS), Zürich, May.

International Energy Agency (1995), *Review of Switzerland,* Paris.

Jans A. and R. Meili (1988), *Rationalisierung der öffentlichen Verwaltung in der Schweiz,* Verlag NZZ, Zurich.

Jeanrenaud, C. (1988), "Gestion publique ou gestion privée des services municipaux: Quelques réflexions sur les pratiques des communes suisses", in CIRIEC, *Les systèmes d'économie mixte dans les économies modernes,* Compte rendu du XVIIe congrès international du CIRIEC, Bordeaux, 19-21 September, pp. 81-94.

King, R.G. and S.T. Rebello (1989), "Low frequency filtering and real business cycles", *Rochester University Centre for Economic Research Working Paper No. 205,* October.

Lehmann, B. (1993), "Lenkungsabgaben auf Dünger – Entscheidungselemente für die Einführung von Lenkungsabgaben auf Mineraldünger und Hofdüngerüberschüsse", Schriftenreihe Institut für Agrarwirtschaft ETH – Zürich, No. 5, December.

Leu, R.E., A. Gemperle, M. Haas and St. Spycher (1993), *Privatisierung auf kantonaler und kommunaler Ebene,* Haupt, Bern.

Manzini, A. (1995), "Visite guidée des privatisations", *Le Mois,* Société des Banques Suisses, Basel, January-February.

OECD (1987), *Economic Survey of Switzerland 1986-87,* Paris.

OECD (1990), *Economic Survey of Switzerland 1989-90,* Paris.

OECD (1995), *Communication Outlook,* Paris.

OECD (1995), *Government in transition, Public Management Reforms in OECD countries,* Paris.

Office fédéral de l'énergie (1995), *Ouverture du marché suisse de l'électricité,* Rapport Cattin, Bern.

Office fédéral de la statistique (1995), *Les transports publics 1993,* Bern.

Office fédéral des questions conjoncturelles (1994), *Marktwirtschaftliche Reformen,* Étude No. 19, Bern.

Pestieau, P. (1993), "Performance and competition in services", in *Market Services and European Integration,* European Economy, No. 3, pp. 125-148.

Peytrignet, M. (1995), "Analyse statistique de l'aggrégat monétaire M1, définition 1995", *Monnaie et conjoncture,* Bulletin trimestriel de la Banque nationale suisse, March.

Pommerehne, W. (1976), "Private versus öffentliche Müllabfuhr: ein theoretischer und empirischer Vergleich", *Finanzarchiv N.F. 35,* pp. 272-294.

Pommerehne, W. (1983), "Private versus öffentliche Müllabfuhr – nochmals betrachtet", *Finanzarchiv N.F. 41,* pp. 466-475.

Publications de la Commission suisse des cartels et du préposé à la surveillance des prix (1995), *État de la concurrence sur certains marchés des déchets,* Bern, February.

Rey, J.N. (1993), "La Poste suisse: des réformes pour bâtir un avenir prospère", *La Vie économique,* September.

Rich, G. (1992), "Die schweizerische Teuerung: Lehren für die Nationalbank", *Monnaie et conjoncture,* Bulletin trimestriel de la Banque nationale suisse, March.

Rosenberg, F. (1993), "La philosophie d'entreprise de Télécom PTT", *La Vie économique,* July.

Schips, B. (1995), "Okonomische Argumente für wirksamen Wettbewerb auch im Versicherungszweig 'Gebäudefeuer- und Gebäudeelementarschäden", St. Gall, January.

Schmid, H. (1993), *Eurostratégie de La Poste: rapport final des PTT,* University of St. Gallen.

Schnewlin, Matthias and Werner Weber (1994), "Preiswirkungen der Mehrwertsteuer", *Konjunktur,* Monatsbericht der KOF/ETH, 12/1994.

Schwab, Nathalie and Laurent Christie (1990), "Réduire le coût des services publics par le choix du mode de fourniture le plus approprié", in: Claude Jeanrenaud and Wim Moesen (eds.), *Gérer l'austérité budgétaire,* Paris.

Sheldon, G. (1994), "Nichtparametrische Messung des technischen Fortschrittes im Schweizer Banksektor", *Revue suisse d'économie politique et statistique,* Vol. 130 (4), December, pp. 691-708.

Syz, D.M. (1994), "Les PTT, de la régie d'État à l'entreprise de pointe", *La Vie économique,* May.

Von Ungern-Stemberg, Th. (1994), "Die kantonalen Gebäudeversicherungen, eine ökonomische Analyse", Cahier No. 9405, deep, Université de Lausanne, June.

Witschard, J.-P. (1995), "Les budgets de la Confédération, des cantons et des communes pour l'année 1995", *La vie économique,* March.

Wright, V. (1994), "Industrial privatization in Western Europe: pressures, problems and paradoxes", in V. Wright (ed.), *Privatization in Western Europe,* Pinter Publishers, London, pp. 1-43.

Zarin-Nejadan, M. (1989), "La fiscalité, le coût d'usage du capital et l'investissement physique privé en Suisse: Une analyse empirique", *Konjunktur,* Special issue.

Zumstein, M. (1994), "Passage à la TVA", *Cahiers de questions conjoncturelles,* No. 4.

Annex

Calendar of main economic events

1994

February

In a national referendum, the people and the cantons approve a constitutional amendment providing for the continuation of the fee (the ''vignette'') for the use of motorways and a special levy on trucks to 2004. Swiss voters also endorse an initiative which will ban transalpine freight trucks and make freight transit by rail compulsory; these measures will come into effect in ten years time. The proposal also bans road construction which would boost transit capacity.

The Federal Council submits to Parliament a proposal to amend the law on labour in industry, trade and commerce. The draft law envisages equal treatment of men and women with respect to worktime, especially work on Sundays and at night, improved protection for night workers and more flexibility on worktime.

April

The National Bank lowers the discount rate from 4.0 to 3.5 per cent.

May

The Federal Council submits to Parliament a draft law on the conversion of technical, commercial and arts-oriented schools into higher-level schools (hautes écoles spécialisées) aimed at better integrating applied research, theoretical training and work experience.

The Federal Council proposes to Parliament a partial revision of the law on land use, primarily with a view to simplifying and speeding up administrative and legal procedures.

The Federal Council submits to Parliament a proposed amendment of the federal law on unfair competition to provide greater scope for clearance sales.

June

Parliament decides to continue to provide subsidised loans to economically weak regions. This decision remains in force until 30 June 1996.

The Federal Council adopts a second set of reforms within the context of the revitalisation programme. The new package of reforms concerns infrastructure, agriculture and public sector issues.

September

Parliament approves a free trade agreement with the three Baltic states.

October

Parliament approves the tenth revision of the old-age and survivors' insurance scheme (AVS). This revision raises the retirement age for women from 62 to 64 (the retirement age for men remains 65) and provides for the years spent by women raising their children to be taken into account in calculating their entitlements.

Parliament approves the amendments of the federal law on the direct federal tax and the harmonisation of direct taxes of cantons and communes.

The Federal Council submits to Parliament a budget consolidation programme (measures d'assainissement 1994) to reduce the structural budget deficit of the Confederation by nearly SF 4 billion by 1998. In this context, the Federal Council seeks Parliament's approval for savings which mainly concern social welfare expenditures, and for tax increases, notably with respect to petrol and fuel taxes.

November

The Federal Council submits to Parliament proposals concerning the promotion of sciences in 1996-99; the envisaged financing amounts to SF 3.9 billion.

The Federal Council proposes to Parliament a revision of the federal law on cartels and on other restrictions to competition. The draft law is still based on the "abuse principle". However, "hard cartels" which set prices, restrict the volume of goods and services for purchase or supply or divide up the market on a territorial basis will be prohibited. The law also envisages the introduction of preventive merger control.

December

The reform law on sickness insurance, which puts the financing of sickness insurance on a sounder footing, enhances competition between insurers and contains cost-control measures, is approved by the people in a referendum. The law is expected to come into force on 1 January 1996.

The Federal Council approves of expenditures of SF 554 million for participation in the research- and education projects of the European Union.

Parliament ratifies the GATT/WTO agreements of the Uruguay Round.

The National Bank sets a second medium-term growth target for the seasonally-adjusted monetary base of 1 per cent per year from end-1994 to end-1999, the same as the first medium-term base money target. The starting point is set below the end-point of the previous target path to take account of the structural decline in base money demand in recent years. As the introduction of VAT is expected to raise the price level, the target for growth in base money in 1995 is set exceptionally at 2 per cent.

Parliament adopts the 1995 budget of the Confederation with minor cuts in expenditures. Compared with the level budgeted for 1994, Confederation expenditures are projected to decline by 0.4 per cent and receipts to grow by 2.0 per cent in 1995, which is in both cases less than the projected growth in nominal GDP. This federal deficit is projected to be SF 6.1 billion (1½ per cent of GDP) in 1995.

Parliament tightens regulations concerning unemployment benefits. From 1 January 1995, benefits are payable only after the first five days of unemployment, and, subject to certain conditions, any job must be accepted after four months of unemployment, otherwise claimants' benefits will be reduced. The ceiling on emoluments for unemployment contributions is raised from SF 97 000 to SF 243 000 per year, and the Federal Council increased contribution rates from the current 2 per cent to 3 per cent.

1995

January

Value added tax, levied at 2 and 6.5 per cent, replaces the turnover tax on goods.

The government decides to redraft in the course of one year the law against money laundering, as a consequence of the rejection of a first version by the Swiss Bankers' Association.

February

The Federal Banking Law, which complies with relevant EU directives, comes into effect. As a consequence of the revision, the National Bank drops the authorisation requirement for foreign borrowers in the Swiss market; bank reporting is now compulsory only for Swiss-franc-denominated bond issues.

March

The National Bank lowers the discount rate from 3.5 to 3.0 per cent.

STATISTICAL ANNEX AND STRUCTURAL INDICATORS

Table A. **Selected background statistics**

	Average 1985-94	1985	1986	1987	1988	1989	1990	1991	1992	1993	1994
A. Percentage change from previous year at constant 1980 prices											
Private consumption	1.4	1.4	2.8	2.1	2.1	2.2	1.5	1.5	-0.2	-0.8	1.3
Gross fixed capital formation	3.2	5.3	7.9	7.4	6.9	5.8	2.6	-2.5	-5.0	-3.1	6.5
Construction	2.4	3.0	4.2	5.4	6.4	6.9	1.9	-3.1	-2.3	-2.8	4.6
Machinery and equipment	4.8	10.4	15.4	11.3	7.9	3.9	3.7	-1.2	-9.6	-3.7	10.1
GDP	1.9	3.7	2.9	2.0	2.9	3.9	2.3	0.0	-0.3	-0.9	2.1
GDP price deflator	3.4	3.1	3.8	2.6	2.4	4.2	5.7	5.5	2.6	2.1	1.7
Industrial production	3.1	5.0	3.9	0.6	8.9	2.6	2.7	0.5	-0.7	-0.5	7.9
Employment	0.2	1.9	1.4	1.2	1.2	1.1	1.3	-0.1	-2.2	-2.6	-1.4
Compensation of employees (current prices)	5.2	6.0	6.1	4.9	5.9	6.9	8.9	7.3	3.4	1.0	1.2
Productivity (real GDP/employment)	1.7	1.7	1.4	0.9	1.7	2.7	1.0	0.1	2.0	1.8	3.6
Unit labour cost (compensation/real GDP)	3.2	2.2	3.1	2.8	2.9	2.9	6.4	7.4	3.7	1.9	-0.9
B. Percentage ratios											
Gross fixed capital formation as per cent of GDP at constant prices	28.0	25.4	26.6	28.0	29.1	29.6	29.7	29.0	27.6	27.0	28.2
Stockbuilding as per cent of GDP at constant prices	1.1	0.6	2.0	2.3	1.4	2.0	2.1	1.2	-0.7	-1.0	0.7
Foreign balance as per cent of GDP at constant prices	-4.5	-1.8	-4.5	-6.2	-6.1	-6.3	-6.3	-5.8	-2.7	-1.7	-3.9
Compensation of employees as per cent of GDP at current prices	60.9	60.7	60.3	60.4	60.7	60.0	60.4	61.5	62.2	62.0	60.4
Direct taxes as per cent of household disposable income	18.0	18.1	18.8	17.9	18.1	17.5	18.0	17.2	17.7	17.6	18.6
Household saving as per cent of disposable income	10.3	5.7	7.0	8.4	9.9	11.0	12.2	13.0	12.7	12.0	11.1
Unemployment as per cent of total labour force	1.7	0.9	0.8	0.7	0.6	0.5	0.5	1.1	2.5	4.5	4.7
C. Other indicator											
Current balance ($ billion)	10.6	5.0	6.9	7.6	9.0	7.0	8.6	10.6	15.1	18.3	18.1

Source: OECD, *National Accounts.*

Table B. Gross national product

Million Swiss francs, current prices

	1985	1986	1987	1988	1989	1990	1991	1992	1993	1994
Private consumption	140 555	144 925	150 210	156 970	166 150	177 650	190 490	198 070	202 325	206 510
Public consumption[1]	30 880	32 325	33 025	35 405	38 485	42 850	46 640	49 320	49 725	50 875
Gross fixed asset formation	54 200	58 995	64 370	71 480	79 860	84 545	84 810	80 375	77 020	80 845
Change in stocks[2]	1 365	4 370	4 975	3 355	6 435	7 310	4 545	–980	–3 190	800
Domestic demand	227 000	240 615	252 580	267 210	290 930	312 355	326 485	326 785	325 880	339 030
Exports of goods and services	89 015	89 115	90 525	97 990	110 510	115 050	116 720	122 170	124 995	127 795
Imports of goods and services	88 065	86 380	88 420	96 790	111 080	113 415	112 130	110 190	107 830	110 660
Gross domestic product at market prices	227 950	243 350	254 685	268 410	290 360	313 990	331 075	338 765	343 045	356 165
Factor income from abroad	21 250	20 595	20 900	24 185	28 010	28 130	29 285	27 715	29 195	..
less: Factor income paid abroad	7 845	9 020	9 495	9 645	13 200	14 535	14 970	14 285	15 110	..
Gross national product at market prices	241 355	254 925	266 090	282 950	305 170	327 585	345 390	352 195	357 130	..

1. Including private social security.
2. Including statistical discrepancy.
Source: Office fédéral de la statistique.

133

Table C. **Gross national product**

Million Swiss francs, 1980 prices

	1985	1986	1987	1988	1989	1990	1991	1992	1993	1994
Private consumption	113 665	116 870	119 290	121 845	124 560	126 430	128 285	128 065	127 030	128 695
Public consumption[1]	24 735	25 650	26 115	27 235	28 365	29 695	30 150	30 105	29 605	30 020
Gross fixed asset formation	46 260	49 910	53 620	57 340	60 650	62 210	60 685	57 640	55 865	59 510
Change in stocks[2]	1 155	3 805	4 335	2 715	4 105	4 335	2 455	-1 455	-2 035	1 425
Domestic demand	185 815	196 235	203 360	209 135	217 680	222 670	221 575	214 355	210 465	219 650
Exports of goods and services	74 170	74 445	75 695	80 090	84 090	86 630	86 005	88 890	90 045	93 560
Imports of goods and services	77 500	82 965	87 530	92 145	97 080	99 905	98 245	94 545	93 595	101 870
Gross domestic product at market prices	182 485	187 715	191 525	197 080	204 690	209 395	209 335	208 700	206 915	211 340
Factor income from abroad	18 935	17 665	17 415	18 810	19 520	20 570	19 855	17 675	17 650	..
less: Factor income paid abroad	7 185	8 790	9 475	9 180	12 200	12 620	11 985	10 775	11 135	..
Gross national product at market prices	194 235	196 590	199 465	206 710	212 010	217 345	217 205	215 600	213 430	..

1. Includes private social security.
2. Including statistical discrepancy.
Source: Office fédéral de la statistique.

134

Table D. **Producer and import prices**

May 1993 = 100

	1992	1993 [1]	1994	1994				1995
				Q1	Q2	Q3	Q4	Q1
Producer price index								
Total	99.5	99.9	99.5	99.3	99.3	99.6	99.6	99.6
Agricultural products		101.9	101.3	101.7	100.4	101.9	101.0	97.5
Manufacturing	99.5	99.7	99.1	99.0	99.0	99.3	99.3	99.6
Food and tobacco		100.3	100.1	100.1	100.2	100.4	99.5	99.4
Textiles and clothing		100.0	100.5	99.9	100.4	100.8	100.8	100.3
Paper and paper products		98.9	97.8	97.4	97.3	97.8	98.8	100.2
Petroleum products		96.7	90.4	90.6	90.3	90.8	90.0	90.3
Chemicals		99.2	95.5	96.6	95.7	95.1	94.5	93.5
Machinery		99.9	99.6	99.8	99.7	99.7	99.3	99.3
Transport equipment		100.4	101.6	100.1	102.0	102.0	102.1	102.1
Furniture and other articles		101.9	103.1	103.1	103.8	102.6	102.9	104.1
Electricity and gas		100.4	101.2	101.2	101.0	101.2	101.6	102.5
Domestic market		100.0	99.9	99.7	99.7	100.1	100.1	100.2
Exports		99.7	98.8	98.8	98.7	98.8	98.7	98.7
Raw materials		103.3	104.7	105.5	105.2	105.3	102.9	99.0
Semi-finished goods		99.6	98.9	98.6	98.6	99.1	99.3	99.6
Consumer goods		99.8	99.8	99.7	99.6	99.8	99.8	100.0
Capital goods		99.9	99.5	99.7	99.4	99.4	99.4	99.4
Import price index	100.2	99.8	99.8	98.9	99.4	100.5	100.2	100.3
Raw materials		104.8	121.5	110.0	116.2	130.1	129.8	132.1
Semi-finished goods		99.6	100.1	98.4	99.5	100.2	102.3	105.1
Consumer goods		99.9	98.6	98.9	98.6	99.0	98.0	97.5
Capital goods		98.4	95.4	97.0	96.4	94.9	93.2	92.5
Total supply price index	99.7	99.9	99.6	99.2	99.3	99.9	99.8	100.0
Raw materials		103.8	111.0	107.2	109.3	114.5	112.8	111.3
Semi-finished goods		99.6	99.2	98.6	98.8	99.4	99.9	100.7
Consumer goods		99.6	99.3	99.3	99.2	99.5	99.1	99.0
Capital goods		99.3	97.9	98.7	98.2	97.7	97.1	96.8

1. As from May 1993, the wholesale price index has been replaced by the total supply price index, which is the total of the producer price and the import price indices. Therefore indices for 1993 are the averages for May to December.
Source: Office fédéral de la statistique, *Indice des prix à la production et à l'importation.*

Table E. **Money supply**

Million Swiss francs, yearly average

	1985	1986	1987	1988	1989	1990	1991	1992	1993	1994
1985 Definition										
Monetary base	31 689	32 270	33 403	31 521	29 910	28 934	29 247	29 056	29 498	30 070
Money supply M1	63 210	66 354	71 351	81 480	77 032	73 775	74 687	74 626	81 597	86 350
Money supply M2	119 182	126 168	138 502	149 097	179 036	202 337	208 882	209 996	193 476	189 868
Money supply M3	259 599	277 146	303 392	333 089	353 719	362 145	373 669	384 063	402 446	424 912
1995 Definition										
Monetary base	31 689	32 270	33 403	31 521	29 910	28 934	29 247	29 056	29 498	30 070
Money supply M1	92 118	98 359	107 906	122 558	117 535	111 570	113 744	116 011	128 212	135 395
Money supply M2	202 292	215 434	233 704	262 078	247 180	227 520	231 370	237 861	276 200	303 518
Money supply M3	258 263	275 248	300 855	329 695	349 184	356 083	365 565	373 230	387 908	406 731

Source: Banque nationale suisse, *Bulletin mensuel.*

136

Table F. Interest rates and capital markets

Million Swiss francs and percentages

	1991	1992	1993	1994	1993 Q1	1993 Q2	1993 Q3	1993 Q4	1994 Q1	1994 Q2	1994 Q3	1994 Q4	1995 Q1
Interest rates (average for the period)													
Discount rate (end of period)	7.0	6.0	4.0	3.5	5.0	5.0	4.5	4.0	4.0	3.5	3.5	3.5	3.0
Three-month deposits (Zurich)	7.6	7.2	4.3	3.5	4.8	4.5	4.1	3.8	3.5	3.6	3.6	3.5	3.2
Government bond yield	6.2	6.4	4.6	4.9	5.0	4.7	4.4	4.1	4.3	4.9	5.3	5.3	5.2
Savings deposits of cantonal banks	5.1	5.1	4.4	3.4	5.1	4.6	4.1	3.9	3.5	3.4	3.3	3.3	3.3
Memorandum items :													
Euro-dollar, three-month	5.9	3.8	3.2	4.6	3.2	3.1	3.1	3.3	3.4	4.3	4.8	5.8	6.2
Euro-bond yields (dollars)	8.2	6.8	6.1	7.0	6.5	6.1	5.9	5.8	5.8	7.1	7.3	7.9	7.9
Capital market													
Foreign bonds	31 931	25 196	45 121	36 872	8 601	9 924	13 379	13 217	14 850	4 372	9 580	8 088	8 442
Domestic bonds	17 631	25 793	34 909	25 337	14 190	3 149	8 723	8 847	9 389	4 571	5 533	5 665	..
Public market issues [1]	16 202	24 558	32 757	24 793	12 939	3 021	8 529	8 269	9 298	4 496	5 407	5 593	6 362
of which:													
Government	4 332	12 286	15 793	11 167	5 841	1 825	4 064	4 064	4 684	1 749	1 907	2 826	3 029
Financial Institutions [2]	9 663	8 624	11 786	10 530	4 915	723	2 718	3 431	3 214	2 472	2 729	2 114	2 741
Other private	2 207	3 648	5 178	3 097	2 183	473	1 747	775	1 399	274	771	653	593
Shares													
Public market issues	1 899	2 598	3 286	2 406	102	537	1 610	1 037	1 076	618	620	91	709
Redemptions	11 419	18 474	30 205	32 743	6 631	7 126	6 613	9 835	9 357	9 398	7 016	6 972	4 825

1. According to date of payment.
2. Including holding companies.
Source: Banque nationale suisse, *Bulletin mensuel*, and OECD, *Financial Statistics*.

137

Table G. **Foreign trade by area**

Million US dollars

	1986	1987	1988	1989	1990	1991	1992	1993	1994
					Exports, fob				
OECD countries	29 500	36 030	40 389	41 243	51 260	49 544	52 801	49 608	55 029
EU	23 055	28 456	31 873	32 526	40 768	39 683	42 372	39 426	43 496
of which: Germany	7 999	9 871	10 916	10 718	14 046	14 580	15 357	14 483	16 408
Other OECD	6 446	7 574	8 517	8 717	10 492	9 861	10 429	10 182	11 532
of which: USA	3 560	4 005	4 344	4 589	5 080	5 038	5 593	5 636	6 428
Non-OECD countries	7 746	9 220	10 225	10 268	12 273	11 786	12 731	13 527	15 036
CEEC	990	1 249	1 354	1 412	1 628	1 330	1 304	1 121	1 359
OPEC	1 697	1 888	1 989	1 592	1 979	2 078	2 365	2 443	2 102
Other	5 060	6 083	6 882	7 264	8 666	8 378	9 062	9 963	11 575
Total	37 247	45 250	50 614	51 511	63 533	61 330	65 531	63 135	70 065
					Imports, cif				
OECD countries	37 178	45 455	50 666	52 418	62 713	59 424	59 550	54 974	61 356
EU	32 512	39 714	43 923	45 099	54 388	50 738	51 555	47 923	53 766
of which: Germany	13 562	17 383	19 263	19 589	23 492	21 711	21 962	19 794	22 232
Other OECD	4 666	5 740	6 743	7 319	8 325	8 685	7 994	7 051	7 590
of which: USA	2 212	2 687	3 125	3 723	4 269	4 867	4 191	3 921	4 479
Non-OECD countries	3 687	4 955	5 644	5 780	6 833	6 847	6 115	5 819	6 355
CEEC	736	641	582	633	671	922	651	434	535
OPEC	615	715	604	328	851	912	656	720	834
Other	2 337	3 599	4 458	4 820	5 311	5 013	4 808	4 664	4 987
Total	40 865	50 410	56 310	58 199	69 546	66 271	65 665	60 794	67 711

Source: OECD, *Foreign Trade Statistics, Series A.*

138

Table H. Foreign trade by commodity group

Million US dollars

	1985	1986	1987	1988	1989	1990	1991	1992	1993
	Exports, fob								
0. Food and live animals	731	982	1 154	1 144	1 142	1 407	1 392	1 493	1 497
1. Beverages and tobacco	138	188	228	258	255	359	377	416	396
2. Crude materials, inedible, except fuels	383	457	526	664	678	740	671	706	655
3. Mineral fuels, lubricants and related materials	91	65	62	69	57	83	127	104	116
4. Animal and vegetable oils and fats	18	17	19	18	20	24	23	22	20
5. Chemicals	5 879	8 137	9 976	11 045	10 912	13 653	13 476	15 303	15 658
6. Manufactured goods, classified chiefly by material	5 572	7 370	8 732	10 101	10 211	12 352	11 362	11 654	11 081
7. Machinery and transport equipment	8 546	12 249	15 045	16 436	16 066	20 519	19 360	20 049	18 752
8. Miscellaneous manufactured articles	5 892	8 095	9 548	10 625	11 739	15 386	14 242	15 451	15 694
9. Commodities and transactions, not classified according to kind	35	36	72	271	360	476	446	417	469
Total	27 284	37 595	45 361	50 632	51 441	64 997	61 477	65 616	64 339
	Imports, cif								
0. Food and live animals	1 949	2 536	2 960	3 037	2 859	3 399	3 381	3 453	3 318
1. Beverages and tobacco	392	531	651	715	726	906	884	833	785
2. Crude materials, inedible, except fuels	1 039	1 273	1 484	1 644	1 672	1 896	1 637	1 613	1 470
3. Mineral fuels, lubricants and related materials	3 074	2 421	2 252	2 086	2 318	3 235	3 105	2 838	2 447
4. Animal and vegetable oils and fats	64	66	56	55	54	69	62	73	77
5. Chemicals	3 665	4 798	5 721	6 675	6 617	7 954	7 617	8 332	8 324
6. Manufactured goods, classified chiefly by material	6 476	8 993	10 994	12 291	13 270	15 412	13 766	13 306	12 781
7. Machinery and transport equipment	7 974	12 225	15 975	18 187	18 250	22 353	21 122	20 213	18 321
8. Miscellaneous manufactured articles	5 822	8 275	10 415	11 443	11 991	14 899	14 235	14 480	13 819
9. Commodities and transactions, not classified according to kind	179	80	50	192	379	520	480	462	508
Total	30 632	41 197	50 557	56 323	58 135	70 645	66 288	65 603	61 849

Source: OECD, *Foreign Trade Statistics,* Series C.

Table I. Balance of payments

Million US dollars

	1985	1986	1987	1988	1989	1990	1991	1992	1993	1994
Exports, fob	28 100	38 470	46 685	52 258	53 182	65 594	63 373	67 799	65 446	72 892
Imports, fob[1]	30 070	40 456	49 789	55 449	57 304	68 833	65 509	65 060	60 321	67 352
Trade balance	-1 970	-1 986	-3 104	-3 191	-4 122	-3 239	-2 136	2 739	5 125	5 540
Services, net	7 812	9 943	12 165	13 948	12 828	14 207	15 325	15 334	16 029	15 926
of which:										
Investment income	6 754	8 499	10 506	13 343	12 691	14 756	15 287	14 893	14 423	14 240
Other factor income	1 058	1 444	1 659	605	137	-549	38	441	1 606	1 686
Balance on goods and services	5 842	7 957	9 061	10 757	8 706	10 968	13 189	18 073	21 154	21 466
Private transfers, net	-841	-1 206	-1 550	-1 712	-1 666	-2 184	-2 275	-2 375	-2 227	-2 644
Official transfers, net	35	116	45	-2	-18	-146	-346	-624	-633	-751
Current balance	5 036	6 867	7 556	9 043	7 022	8 638	10 568	15 074	18 294	18 071
Balance on non-monetary transactions	704	5 757	4 295	-8 940	-16 911	-9 183	-4 092	9 050	227	..
Private monetary institutions' short-term capital	467	-4 704	-1 165	6 577	18 388	10 387	5 052	-4 628	188	..
Assets (− = increase)	-4 881	-10 167	-13 407	3 174	8 854	-2 125	1984	-4 616	-2 220	..
Liabilities	5 348	5 463	12 243	3 404	9 534	12 511	3 068	-12	2 407	..
Balance on official settlements[2]	1 171	1 053	3 130	-2 363	1 477	1 204	960	4 422	415	..
Special transactions	..	..	..	..	..	..	..	..	..	..
Miscellaneous official accounts	-1 456	-2 045	-2 284	1 361	839	-2 929	1 154	408	566	..
Change in reserves (+ = increase)	-284	-992	846	-1 001	2 316	-1 727	2 111	4 829	980	..
Gold	..	..	..	..	..	..	..	..	..	..
Currency assets[3]	-126	-773	1 071	-884	2 344	-1 672	2 108	4 002	794	..
Reserve position in IMF	-152	-215	-237	-125	-86	-47	0	814	134	..
Special Drawing Rights	-7	-4	12	8	57	-8	3	13	52	..

1. Imports cif minus 5 per cent as estimate for freight and insurance.
2. Central Bank liabilities and other assets.
3. Including Roosa-bonds held by the Confederation.
Source: Banque national suisse, *Bulletin mensuel*, and OECD estimates.

Table J. **Gross value added by main area of activity**

	1975	1985	1990	1975	1985	1990
	SF million			As a percentage of GDP		
Enterprises	124 685	203 930	280 051	89.0	89.5	89.2
Non-financial enterprises	116 282	180 832	250 681	83.0	79.3	79.8
Agriculture, forestry	6 487	8 180	9 664	4.6	3.6	3.1
Energy, metal ore mining	2 808	5 023	6 011	2.0	2.2	1.9
Industrial arts and crafts	41 687	58 794	76 722	29.7	25.8	24.4
Building and civil engineering	11 210	17 325	26 224	8.0	7.6	8.4
Distributive trades, hotels and catering, repairs	29 430	44 689	62 343	21.0	19.6	19.9
Transport and communications	9 140	14 550	18 556	6.5	6.4	5.9
Real estate and consultancy services	5 946	15 100	26 324	4.2	6.6	8.4
Rental and dwellings	5 290	9 878	13 949	3.8	4.3	4.4
Other services	4 284	7 293	10 887	3.1	3.2	3.5
Banking and insurance	8 403	23 096	29 370	6.0	10.1	9.4
Government and social insurance	14 452	26 065	37 070	10.3	11.4	11.8
Household and private non-profit institutions	2 453	4 655	6 783	1.8	2.0	2.2
Total (unadjusted)	141 590	234 650	323 903	101.1	102.9	103.2
Adjustments						
Imputed value of bank service charge	-4 565	-10 400	-14 180	-3.3	-4.6	-4.5
Import duties	3 130	3 700	4 267	2.2	1.6	1.4
Adjusted total = gross domestic product	140 155	227 950	313 990	100.0	100.0	100.0

Source: Office fédéral de la statistique, *National Accounts.*

141

Table K. **Labour market: structural and institutional characteristics**

	1975	1980	1985	1990	1991	1992	1993	1994
Labour force (thousand)	3 118	3 172	3 382	3 583	3 600	3 573	3 552	3 501
of which: Foreigners,[1] end-August	754	706	756	955	989	977	950	947
Participation rate[2] (per cent)								
Total	74.8	74.4	75.5	78.1	77.6	76.3	75.4	..
Male	97.7	94.5	94.4	96.4	95.4	93.9	92.8	..
Female	51.9	54.1	56.2	59.7	59.7	58.6	57.9	..
Employment/labour force	74.5	74.2	74.5	77.6	76.8	74.3	71.9	..
Employment by sector								
Agriculture	7.6	6.9	6.1	5.6	5.5	5.6	5.6	5.7
Industry	42.2	38.1	35.6	35.0	34.4	33.9	33.2	32.7
Services	50.2	55.0	58.3	59.5	60.1	60.5	61.2	61.6
Wholly unemployed (thousand)	..	6.3	27.0	16.0	35.6	82.4	145.0	150.0
of which: Foreigners (per cent of total)	..	..	33.1	42.7	44.3	40.9	40.2	45.5
Unemployment rate	0.3	0.2	1.0	0.5	1.1	2.5	4.5	4.7
Vacancies								
Full-time[3]	..	12 312	7 875	16 711	10 145	7 741	5 370	4 776
Part-time	..	..	647	550	404	425	373	449
Number of days not worked (lock-out and strikes)	1 733	5 178	662	4 090	51	673	..	..

1. Includes settled workers, workers on a one-year contract and seasonal and border workers.
2. Labour force as a percentage of the corresponding population aged 15-64.
3. The decomposition between full and part-time begins in 1983, so for 1980 it is total vacancies.
Source: Office fédéral de la statistique, *Annuaire statistique de la Suisse,* 1995; Département fédéral de l'économie publique, *La vie économique,* and OECD, *Labour Force Statistics.*

Table L. **The structure of taxation**

Per cent of GDP

	1980	1985	1989	1990	1991	1992	1993
Tax receipts	30.8	32.1	31.7	31.5	31.2	31.8	33.1
Personal income tax	11.0	11.2	10.6	10.8	10.7	11.1	10.9
Corporate tax	1.8	1.9	2.0	2.1	2.0	2.0	1.9
Social security tax	9.5	10.3	10.4	10.4	10.7	11.0	12.4
Property taxes	2.2	2.6	2.8	2.5	2.2	2.3	2.4
Tax on goods and services	6.3	6.1	5.9	5.8	5.6	5.4	5.5
Memorandum:							
Income tax as a per cent of total tax	41.6	40.8	39.7	40.8	40.7	41.2	38.7

Source: OECD, *Revenue Statistics of OECD Member Countries,* 1965-1993.

143

Table M. **Interest rate margins in banking**[1]

Per cent of average balance sheet total

	1981	1988	1989	1990	1991	1992	1993
Large banks	1.10	1.36	1.37	1.24	1.52	1.68	1.92
Cantonal banks	1.00	1.13	1.13	1.22	1.34	1.34	1.48
Regional and saving banks	1.30	1.21	1.20	1.32	1.48	1.51	1.51
Loans associations and agricultural credit co-operatives	1.00	0.95	0.96	1.04	1.13	1.14	1.19
Other Swiss and foreign banks	2.00	1.98	2.05	2.01	2.11	2.13	2.48

1. Interest received less interest paid.
Source: OECD, *Bank Profitability (Statistical Supplement), Financial Statements of Banks, 1984-93,* 1995.

BASIC STATISTICS:

INTERNATIONAL COMPARISONS

	Units	Reference period [1]	Australia	Au
Population				
Total	Thousands	1992	17 489	7
Inhabitants per sq. km	Number	1992	2	
Net average annual increase over previous 10 years	%	1992	1.4	
Employment				
Civilian employment (CE)[2]	Thousands	1992	7 637	3
Of which: Agriculture	% of CE		5.3	
Industry	% of CE		23.8	
Services	% of CE		71	
Gross domestic product (GDP)				
At current prices and current exchange rates	Bill. US$	1992	296.6	18
Per capita	US$		16 959	23
At current prices using current PPPs[3]	Bill. US$	1992	294.5	
Per capita	US$		16 800	18
Average annual volume growth over previous 5 years	%	1992	2	
Gross fixed capital formation (GFCF)	% of GDP	1992	19.7	
Of which: Machinery and equipment	% of GDP		9.3	
Residential construction	% of GDP		5.1	
Average annual volume growth over previous 5 years	%	1992	−1	
Gross saving ratio[4]	% of GDP	1992	15.6	2
General government				
Current expenditure on goods and services	% of GDP	1992	18.5	
Current disbursements[5]	% of GDP	1992	36.9	4
Current receipts	% of GDP	1992	33.1	4
Net official development assistance	% of GNP	1992	0.33	
Indicators of living standards				
Private consumption per capita using current PPPs[3]	US$	1992	10 527	9
Passenger cars, per 1 000 inhabitants	Number	1990	430	
Telephones, per 1 000 inhabitants	Number	1990	448	
Television sets, per 1 000 inhabitants	Number	1989	484	
Doctors, per 1 000 inhabitants	Number	1991	2	
Infant mortality per 1 000 live births	Number	1991	7.1	
Wages and prices (average annual increase over previous 5 years)				
Wages (earnings or rates according to availability)	%	1992	5	
Consumer prices	%	1992	5.2	
Foreign trade				
Exports of goods, fob*	Mill. US$	1992	42 844	44
As % of GDP	%		14.4	2
Average annual increase over previous 5 years	%		10.1	
Imports of goods, cif*	Mill. US$	1992	40 751	54
As % of GDP	%		13.7	
Average annual increase over previous 5 years	%		8.6	
Total official reserves[6]	Mill. SDRs	1992	8 152	9
As ratio of average monthly imports of goods	Ratio		2.4	

* At current prices and exchange rates.
1. Unless otherwise stated.
2. According to the definitions used in OECD *Labour Force Statistics*.
3. PPPs = Purchasing Power Parities.
4. Gross saving = Gross national disposable income minus private and government consumption.
5. Current disbursements = Current expenditure on goods and services plus current transfers and payments of property income.
6. Gold included in reserves is valued at 35 SDRs per ounce. End of year.
7. Including Luxembourg.

EMPLOYMENT OPPORTUNITIES

Economics Department, OECD

The Economics Department of the OECD offers challenging and rewarding opportunities to economists interested in applied policy analysis in an international environment. The Department's concerns extend across the entire field of economic policy analysis, both macroeconomic and microeconomic. Its main task is to provide, for discussion by committees of senior officials from Member countries, documents and papers dealing with current policy concerns. Within this programme of work, three major responsibilities are:

- to prepare regular surveys of the economies of individual Member countries;
- to issue full twice-yearly reviews of the economic situation and prospects of the OECD countries in the context of world economic trends;
- to analyse specific policy issues in a medium-term context for the OECD as a whole, and to a lesser extent for the non-OECD countries.

The documents prepared for these purposes, together with much of the Department's other economic work, appear in published form in the *OECD Economic Outlook, OECD Economic Surveys, OECD Economic Studies* and the Department's *Working Papers* series.

The Department maintains a world econometric model, INTERLINK, which plays an important role in the preparation of the policy analyses and twice-yearly projections. The availability of extensive cross-country data bases and good computer resources facilitates comparative empirical analysis, much of which is incorporated into the model.

The Department is made up of about 80 professional economists from a variety of backgrounds and Member countries. Most projects are carried out by small teams and last from four to eighteen months. Within the Department, ideas and points of view are widely discussed; there is a lively professional interchange, and all professional staff have the opportunity to contribute actively to the programme of work.

Skills the Economics Department is looking for:

a) Solid competence in using the tools of both microeconomic and macroeconomic theory to answer policy questions. Experience indicates that this normally requires the equivalent of a Ph.D. in economics or substantial relevant professional experience to compensate for a lower degree.

b) Solid knowledge of economic statistics and quantitative methods; this includes how to identify data, estimate structural relationships, apply basic techniques of time series analysis, and test hypotheses. It is essential to be able to interpret results sensibly in an economic policy context.

c) A keen interest in and extensive knowledge of policy issues, economic developments and their political/social contexts.

d) Interest and experience in analysing questions posed by policy-makers and presenting the results to them effectively and judiciously. Thus, work experience in government agencies or policy research institutions is an advantage.

e) The ability to write clearly, effectively, and to the point. The OECD is a bilingual organisation with French and English as the official languages. Candidates must have excellent knowledge of one of these languages, and some knowledge of the other. Knowledge of other languages might also be an advantage for certain posts.

f) For some posts, expertise in a particular area may be important, but a successful candidate is expected to be able to work on a broader range of topics relevant to the work of the Department. Thus, except in rare cases, the Department does not recruit narrow specialists.

g) The Department works on a tight time schedule with strict deadlines. Moreover, much of the work in the Department is carried out in small groups. Thus, the ability to work with other economists from a variety of cultural and professional backgrounds, to supervise junior staff, and to produce work on time is important.

General information

The salary for recruits depends on educational and professional background. Positions carry a basic salary from FF 305 700 or FF 377 208 for Administrators (economists) and from FF 438 348 for Principal Administrators (senior economists). This may be supplemented by expatriation and/or family allowances, depending on nationality, residence and family situation. Initial appointments are for a fixed term of two to three years.

Vacancies are open to candidates from OECD Member countries. The Organisation seeks to maintain an appropriate balance between female and male staff and among nationals from Member countries.

For further information on employment opportunities in the Economics Department, contact:

Administrative Unit
Economics Department
OECD
2, rue André-Pascal
75775 PARIS CEDEX 16
FRANCE

E-Mail: compte.esadmin@oecd.org

Applications citing ''ECSUR'', together with a detailed *curriculum vitae* in English or French, should be sent to the Head of Personnel at the above address.

MAIN SALES OUTLETS OF OECD PUBLICATIONS
PRINCIPAUX POINTS DE VENTE DES PUBLICATIONS DE L'OCDE

ARGENTINA – ARGENTINE
Carlos Hirsch S.R.L.
Galería Güemes, Florida 165, 4° Piso
1333 Buenos Aires   Tel. (1) 331.1787 y 331.2391
                    Telefax: (1) 331.1787

AUSTRALIA – AUSTRALIE
D.A. Information Services
648 Whitehorse Road, P.O.B 163
Mitcham, Victoria 3132   Tel. (03) 873.4411
                           Telefax: (03) 873.5679

AUSTRIA – AUTRICHE
Gerold & Co.
Graben 31
Wien I   Tel. (0222) 533.50.14
                      Telefax: (0222) 512.47.31.29

BELGIUM – BELGIQUE
Jean De Lannoy
Avenue du Roi 202 Koningslaan
B-1060 Bruxelles   Tel. (02) 538.51.69/538.08.41
                      Telefax: (02) 538.08.41

CANADA
Renouf Publishing Company Ltd.
1294 Algoma Road
Ottawa, ON K1B 3W8   Tel. (613) 741.4333
                        Telefax: (613) 741.5439
Stores:
61 Sparks Street
Ottawa, ON K1P 5R1   Tel. (613) 238.8985
211 Yonge Street
Toronto, ON M5B 1M4   Tel. (416) 363.3171
                        Telefax: (416)363.59.63

Les Éditions La Liberté Inc.
3020 Chemin Sainte-Foy
Sainte-Foy, PQ G1X 3V6   Tel. (418) 658.3763
                        Telefax: (418) 658.3763

Federal Publications Inc.
165 University Avenue, Suite 701
Toronto, ON M5H 3B8   Tel. (416) 860.1611
                        Telefax: (416) 860.1608

Les Publications Fédérales
1185 Université
Montréal, QC H3B 3A7   Tel. (514) 954.1633
                        Telefax: (514) 954.1635

CHINA – CHINE
China National Publications Import
Export Corporation (CNPIEC)
16 Gongti E. Road, Chaoyang District
P.O. Box 88 or 50
Beijing 100704 PR   Tel. (01) 506.6688
                        Telefax: (01) 506.3101

CHINESE TAIPEI – TAIPEI CHINOIS
Good Faith Worldwide Int'l. Co. Ltd.
9th Floor, No. 118, Sec. 2
Chung Hsiao E. Road
Taipei   Tel. (02) 391.7396/391.7397
                      Telefax: (02) 394.9176

CZECH REPUBLIC – RÉPUBLIQUE
TCHÈQUE
Artia Pegas Press Ltd.
Narodni Trida 25
POB 825
111 21 Praha 1   Tel. 26.65.68
                           Telefax: 26.20.81

DENMARK – DANEMARK
Munksgaard Book and Subscription Service
35, Nørre Søgade, P.O. Box 2148
DK-1016 København K   Tel. (33) 12.85.70
                        Telefax: (33) 12.93.87

EGYPT – ÉGYPTE
Middle East Observer
41 Sherif Street
Cairo   Tel. 392.6919
                           Telefax: 360-6804

FINLAND – FINLANDE
Akateeminen Kirjakauppa
Keskuskatu 1, P.O. Box 128
00100 Helsinki
Subscription Services/Agence d'abonnements :
P.O. Box 23
00371 Helsinki   Tel. (358 0) 121 4416
                        Telefax: (358 0) 121.4450

FRANCE
OECD/OCDE
Mail Orders/Commandes par correspondance:
2, rue André-Pascal
75775 Paris Cedex 16   Tel. (33-1) 45.24.82.00
                      Telefax: (33-1) 49.10.42.76
                      Telex: 640048 OCDE
Internet: Compte.PUBSINQ @ oecd.org
Orders via Minitel, France only/
Commandes par Minitel, France exclusivement :
36 15 OCDE

OECD Bookshop/Librairie de l'OCDE :
33, rue Octave-Feuillet
75016 Paris   Tel. (33-1) 45.24.81.81
                           (33-1) 45.24.81.67

Documentation Française
29, quai Voltaire
75007 Paris   Tel. 40.15.70.00
Gibert Jeune (Droit-Économie)
6, place Saint-Michel
75006 Paris   Tel. 43.25.91.19
Librairie du Commerce International
10, avenue d'Iéna
75016 Paris   Tel. 40.73.34.60
Librairie Dunod
Université Paris-Dauphine
Place du Maréchal de Lattre de Tassigny
75016 Paris   Tel. (1) 44.05.40.13
Librairie Lavoisier
11, rue Lavoisier
75008 Paris   Tel. 42.65.39.95
Librairie L.G.D.J. - Montchrestien
20, rue Soufflot
75005 Paris   Tel. 46.33.89.85
Librairie des Sciences Politiques
30, rue Saint-Guillaume
75007 Paris   Tel. 45.48.36.02
P.U.F.
49, boulevard Saint-Michel
75005 Paris   Tel. 43.25.83.40
Librairie de l'Université
12a, rue Nazareth
13100 Aix-en-Provence   Tel. (16) 42.26.18.08
Documentation Française
165, rue Garibaldi
69003 Lyon   Tel. (16) 78.63.32.23
Librairie Decitre
29, place Bellecour
69002 Lyon   Tel. (16) 72.40.54.54
Librairie Sauramps
Le Triangle
34967 Montpellier Cedex 2 Tel. (16) 67.58.85.15
                        Tekefax: (16) 67.58.27.36

GERMANY – ALLEMAGNE
OECD Publications and Information Centre
August-Bebel-Allee 6
D-53175 Bonn   Tel. (0228) 959.120
                      Telefax: (0228) 959.12.17

GREECE – GRÈCE
Librairie Kauffmann
Mavrokordatou 9
106 78 Athens   Tel. (01) 32.55.321
                        Telefax: (01) 32.30.320

HONG-KONG
Swindon Book Co. Ltd.
Astoria Bldg. 3F
34 Ashley Road, Tsimshatsui
Kowloon, Hong Kong   Tel. 2376.2062
                        Telefax: 2376.0685

HUNGARY – HONGRIE
Euro Info Service
Margitsziget, Európa Ház
1138 Budapest   Tel. (1) 111.62.16
                        Telefax: (1) 111.60.61

ICELAND – ISLANDE
Mál Mog Menning
Laugavegi 18, Pósthólf 392
121 Reykjavik   Tel. (1) 552.4240
                        Telefax: (1) 562.3523

INDIA – INDE
Oxford Book and Stationery Co.
Scindia House
New Delhi 110001   Tel. (11) 331.5896/5308
                      Telefax: (11) 332.5993
17 Park Street
Calcutta 700016   Tel. 240832

INDONESIA – INDONÉSIE
Pdii-Lipi
P.O. Box 4298
Jakarta 12042   Tel. (21) 573.34.67
                        Telefax: (21) 573.34.67

IRELAND – IRLANDE
Government Supplies Agency
Publications Section
4/5 Harcourt Road
Dublin 2   Tel. 661.31.11
                         Telefax: 475.27.60

ISRAEL
Praedicta
5 Shatner Street
P.O. Box 34030
Jerusalem 91430   Tel. (2) 52.84.90/1/2
                      Telefax: (2) 52.84.93

R.O.Y. International
P.O. Box 13056
Tel Aviv 61130   Tel. (3) 546 1423
                        Telefax: (3) 546 1442

Palestinian Authority/Middle East:
INDEX Information Services
P.O.B. 19502
Jerusalem   Tel. (2) 27.12.19
                        Telefax: (2) 27.16.34

ITALY – ITALIE
Libreria Commissionaria Sansoni
Via Duca di Calabria 1/1
50125 Firenze   Tel. (055) 64.54.15
                        Telefax: (055) 64.12.57
Via Bartolini 29
20155 Milano   Tel. (02) 36.50.83
Editrice e Libreria Herder
Piazza Montecitorio 120
00186 Roma   Tel. 679.46.28
                         Telefax: 678.47.51
Libreria Hoepli
Via Hoepli 5
20121 Milano   Tel. (02) 86.54.46
                        Telefax: (02) 805.28.86
Libreria Scientifica
Dott. Lucio de Biasio 'Aeiou'
Via Coronelli, 6
20146 Milano   Tel. (02) 48.95.45.52
                        Telefax: (02) 48.95.45.48

JAPAN – JAPON
OECD Publications and Information Centre
Landic Akasaka Building
2-3-4 Akasaka, Minato-ku
Tokyo 107   Tel. (81.3) 3586.2016
                      Telefax: (81.3) 3584.7929

KOREA – CORÉE
Kyobo Book Centre Co. Ltd.
P.O. Box 1658, Kwang Hwa Moon
Seoul   Tel. 730.78.91
                        Telefax: 735.00.30

MALAYSIA – MALAISIE
University of Malaya Bookshop
University of Malaya
P.O. Box 1127, Jalan Pantai Baru
59700 Kuala Lumpur
Malaysia   Tel. 756.5000/756.5425
                            Telefax: 756.3246

MEXICO – MEXIQUE
Revistas y Periodicos Internacionales S.A. de C.V.
Florencia 57 - 1004
Mexico, D.F. 06600   Tel. 207.81.00
                               Telefax: 208.39.79

NETHERLANDS – PAYS-BAS
SDU Uitgeverij Plantijnstraat
Externe Fondsen
Postbus 20014
2500 EA's-Gravenhage   Tel. (070) 37.89.880
Voor bestellingen: Telefax: (070) 34.75.778

**NEW ZEALAND
NOUVELLE-ZÉLANDE**
GPLegislation Services
P.O. Box 12418
Thorndon, Wellington   Tel. (04) 496.5655
                               Telefax: (04) 496.5698

NORWAY – NORVÈGE
Narvesen Info Center – NIC
Bertrand Narvesens vei 2
P.O. Box 6125 Etterstad
0602 Oslo 6   Tel. (022) 57.33.00
                            Telefax: (022) 68.19.01

PAKISTAN
Mirza Book Agency
65 Shahrah Quaid-E-Azam
Lahore 54000   Tel. (42) 353.601
                            Telefax: (42) 231.730

PHILIPPINE – PHILIPPINES
International Book Center
5th Floor, Filipinas Life Bldg.
Ayala Avenue
Metro Manila   Tel. 81.96.76
                         Telex 23312 RHP PH

PORTUGAL
Livraria Portugal
Rua do Carmo 70-74
Apart. 2681
1200 Lisboa   Tel. (01) 347.49.82/5
                            Telefax: (01) 347.02.64

SINGAPORE – SINGAPOUR
Gower Asia Pacific Pte Ltd.
Golden Wheel Building
41, Kallang Pudding Road, No. 04-03
Singapore 1334   Tel. 741.5166
                            Telefax: 742.9356

SPAIN – ESPAGNE
Mundi-Prensa Libros S.A.
Castelló 37, Apartado 1223
Madrid 28001   Tel. (91) 431.33.99
                            Telefax: (91) 575.39.98

Libreria Internacional AEDOS
Consejo de Ciento 391
08009 – Barcelona   Tel. (93) 488.30.09
                            Telefax: (93) 487.76.59

Llibreria de la Generalitat
Palau Moja
Rambla dels Estudis, 118
08002 – Barcelona
           (Subscripcions) Tel. (93) 318.80.12
           (Publicacions) Tel. (93) 302.67.23
                            Telefax: (93) 412.18.54

SRI LANKA
Centre for Policy Research
c/o Colombo Agencies Ltd.
No. 300-304, Galle Road
Colombo 3   Tel. (1) 574240, 573551-2
                         Telefax: (1) 575394, 510711

SWEDEN – SUÈDE
Fritzes Customer Service
S–106 47 Stockholm   Tel. (08) 690.90.90
                            Telefax: (08) 20.50.21

Subscription Agency/Agence d'abonnements :
Wennergren-Williams Info AB
P.O. Box 1305
171 25 Solna   Tel. (08) 705.97.50
                            Telefax: (08) 27.00.71

SWITZERLAND – SUISSE
Maditec S.A. (Books and Periodicals - Livres
et périodiques)
Chemin des Palettes 4
Case postale 266
1020 Renens VD 1   Tel. (021) 635.08.65
                            Telefax: (021) 635.07.80

Librairie Payot S.A.
4, place Pépinet
CP 3212
1002 Lausanne   Tel. (021) 341.33.47
                            Telefax: (021) 341.33.45

Librairie Unilivres
6, rue de Candolle
1205 Genève   Tel. (022) 320.26.23
                            Telefax: (022) 329.73.18

Subscription Agency/Agence d'abonnements :
Dynapresse Marketing S.A.
38 avenue Vibert
1227 Carouge   Tel. (022) 308.07.89
                            Telefax: (022) 308.07.99

See also – Voir aussi :
OECD Publications and Information Centre
August-Bebel-Allee 6
D-53175 Bonn (Germany)   Tel. (0228) 959.120
                            Telefax: (0228) 959.12.17

THAILAND – THAÏLANDE
Suksit Siam Co. Ltd.
113, 115 Fuang Nakhon Rd.
Opp. Wat Rajbopith
Bangkok 10200   Tel. (662) 225.9531/2
                            Telefax: (662) 222.5188

TURKEY – TURQUIE
Kültür Yayinlari Is-Türk Ltd. Sti.
Atatürk Bulvari No. 191/Kat 13
Kavaklidere/Ankara   Tel. 428.11.40 Ext. 2458
Dolmabahce Cad. No. 29
Besiktas/Istanbul   Tel. (312) 260 7188
                         Telex: (312) 418 29 46

UNITED KINGDOM – ROYAUME-UNI
HMSO
Gen. enquiries   Tel. (171) 873 8496
Postal orders only:
P.O. Box 276, London SW8 5DT
Personal Callers HMSO Bookshop
49 High Holborn, London WC1V 6HB
                            Telefax: (171) 873 8416
Branches at: Belfast, Birmingham, Bristol,
Edinburgh, Manchester

UNITED STATES – ÉTATS-UNIS
OECD Publications and Information Center
2001 L Street N.W., Suite 650
Washington, D.C. 20036-4910 Tel. (202) 785.6323
                            Telefax: (202) 785.0350

VENEZUELA
Libreria del Este
Avda F. Miranda 52, Aptdo. 60337
Edificio Galipán
Caracas 106   Tel. 951.1705/951.2307/951.1297
                         Telegram: Libreste Caracas

Subscription to OECD periodicals may also be
placed through main subscription agencies.

Les abonnements aux publications périodiques de
l'OCDE peuvent être souscrits auprès des
principales agences d'abonnement.

Orders and inquiries from countries where Distribu-
tors have not yet been appointed should be sent to:
OECD Publications Service, 2 rue André-Pascal,
75775 Paris Cedex 16, France.

Les commandes provenant de pays où l'OCDE n'a
pas encore désigné de distributeur peuvent être
adressées à : OCDE, Service des Publications,
2, rue André-Pascal, 75775 Paris Cedex 16, France.

7-1995

PRINTED IN FRANCE

•

OECD PUBLICATIONS
2, rue André-Pascal
75775 PARIS CEDEX 16
No. 48183
(10 95 26 1) ISBN 92-64-14584-2
ISSN 0376-6438

•